Life's Equation

A journey toward finding greater purpose

FRANK DAIDONE

Life's Equation by Frank Daidone

Frank@lifesequation.net, www.lifesequation.net

Library of Congress Cataloging-in-Publication Data:

Copyright © 2016 Frank Daidone

All rights reserved.

ISBN: 1493754475
ISBN-13: 978-1493754472

This book is dedicated to my brother, Anthony.

CONTENTS

ACKNOWLEDGMENTS

It's difficult to truly acknowledge everyone that was instrumental in the creation of this book. My good friend, Alena, has been a tremendous support helping me actually complete this book. He showed me possibilities I never imagined then pushed me along the way. Mark for his insane approach to the world and the gift of letting me see it through his eyes. My children, Camryn and Erin, who have inspired me from the moment I held each of them in my hands for the first time. Over the years they've put themselves aside providing me with the gift of time to accomplish my goals. Most importantly, Ashley, my wife and best friend, for being the light that has guided me in life with encouragement to find the best part of me. She is the reason this book exists. She has made all my dreams come true.

INTRODUCTION

Do you ever ask yourself 'What is my purpose?' or more specifically, do you ever question if you are on the right path? As far back as I can recall I've attempted to make sense of my own purpose in life, accepting only what seemed realistic while disregarding everything else. Most of us subconsciously do this multiple times throughout the stages in our lives and sometimes constantly via the voice inside our head. But we have a tendency to set unsatisfying goals for ourselves because of perceived limitations or to avoid our fears.

As we grow, we often tend to limit our potential and miss out on opportunities as we struggle with doubt and apprehension. Envy, doubt, love and fear are all emotions we adopt through experiences and interactions with other people through this journey called Life –

establishing a profound effect on how we move through the world.

I'm not saying my life experiences are typical – far from it, and if you stick with me through this journey you'll quickly discover what I mean – yet there are common ways in which we all process our experiences, however varied, to shape our beliefs and perspectives. For whatever reason I became determined to find those connections between experience and perspective that would allow me to make choices that were right for me.

For instance, where we are born and into what type of family are key influencers in how we choose our own paths. However, it's our emotional reaction to our situation that tends to shape our decisions. We quickly select a path for ourselves in order to move forward, establishing a perspective that will lead the way toward creating our sense of purpose. That perspective, or view of the world, is critical to self survival and can have a vital effect on us and those around us either positively or negatively. While a clear perspective is unarguably the most critical component for finding one's true purpose, finding that clarity free of clouded judgment and the weight of outside influences can be difficult. If our perspective is determined through emotional experiences with others, how can we clearly know what our true purpose really is?

Successful leaders know not to make emotionally driven decisions. So why do we make these types of decisions for ourselves? The probable answer is that we aren't aware it's happening. The moment we take our first breath outside the womb we are nurtured and guided by our upbringing. Whether affected by our parents' influences, lessons from teachers, our socioeconomic situation or the environment in which we reside, as children we instinctually take action based on what we've learned and how it affected us. As adults we innately continue that process, allowing our emotionally-connected experiences to drive the decisions we make.

This book offers my life under a microscope, highlighting some personal life events through which I began to develop an equation, my own "theory of everything," to help me better navigate what were, at times, some pretty challenging experiences, while freeing my perspective from that emotional misdirection. You'll see how my equation came together – and you'll hear stories about some of the people I met along the way who influenced me in some truly inspiring ways – while helping me to uncover some basic but unexpected truths that I hope in turn will inspire you.

What you are about to read is a revolutionary way to find the clearest perspective on reality using the formula to discover common energy in all living things. While the message is assembled through a collection of significant, sometimes humorous, moving experiences and hard-won lessons, this book ultimately represents a proven equation toward discovering maximum potential, accomplishing goals and making true, raw sense of one's own purpose. Come celebrate your experiences through logically discovering your true purpose – and help make the world a better place in the process.

I

INFORMATION

We are born without form and shaped by every hand that touches us.

We exist within a world of information and through our experience we associate information to create our reality. Our memories are a collection of information and understanding we refer to as "our life." Whether or not our memories have associated imagery, they still define what we accept as real. For example, I don't have a visual memory of touching a hot iron when I was young but I know I did – and that it resulted in pain. That memory is one tiny piece of understanding I added to my reality. *Information provides the building blocks for life.*

My life begins with a simple snapshot memory - no sound, no motion - just a visual. I can see my mother sitting on a black vinyl couch, holding my one-day-old brother, Anthony, swaddled in her arms. In the foreground, I can see my four-year-old hand reaching out to touch him in disbelief that he had finally arrived. That image is frozen in my mind and no other memory precedes it. That memory is the moment I was born.

I grew up on Long Island in New York, where most of my time

was spent surrounded by fresh air, tall trees and a large Italian family. My days consisted of nature walks in my backyard, where I watched blue jays, bugs and dragonflies. Sometimes, if I was lucky, I'd find a salamander under a rock or a turtle perched in our vegetable garden, chewing on a fallen tomato. At night in the front yard, my older sister, Anne and I caught fireflies in the moonlight, while the sound of crickets rang in our ears. My mom would sit on the porch, rocking my brother in her arms while watching over us. I remember those moments as harmonious and carefree based on the reflection I saw in my mother's eyes.

Many of my early memories do not include my dad, since he was off to work before I got up and often returned home after I was in bed. Sometimes I'd hear him come in late at night and he'd ask if I were still up. The few times he came home before I went to bed, he hugged me and said, "I love you."

Each time I just said, "Good night." The odd thing was I loved him very much. I just couldn't bring myself to say, "I love you" to someone I hardly knew.

My father's favorite expression was, "You get what you give." Though my mom would laugh and say, "That doesn't mean anything," it meant something to me and played a key role in shaping my understanding of the world.

My dad was a man of few words, none of which were small talk. And he only spoke if he knew you were listening. I always listened when he spoke because I knew he would say something about being alive. He'd say things like: "Gently touch a rash if you have to, but never scratch." "When you shake a man's hand, you look him square in the eye." "Learning guitar is the greatest gift you can give yourself." "Freedom is a state of mind."

My father achieved many great things during his life, but in my mind his single greatest accomplishment was his undying effort to bring the best possible situation to his family. He did this the only way he knew how, with hard work and by facing every challenge head on. His golden rule for success was, "Either do something no one wants to do or do something no one knows how to do." He chose the latter when he eventually traded the night shift for night school. My dad provided me with the model of a man, a collection of quiet strength and simple wisdom. His words and my memories of him define my childhood and are part of who I am today.

Another vivid snapshot memory from my childhood was when my brother was seven months old. I see my mother standing motionless inside our front doorway, holding my brother in her arms. Her eyes were wide and my father was next to her with his hand resting on her shoulder. They had just returned from a doctor's visit where they were informed that my brother had severe cerebral palsy, caused by damage to the brain, and would never walk or talk. His life expectancy was only about seven years.

When I picture their faces, I know I'll never comprehend what that must have been like for them, just as they could not then begin to comprehend the struggle standing before them. That night, from my parents' bedroom, I could hear my mother crying in a way I had never heard before. My father's steady voice was laced between her sobs repeating, "Everything will be alright." The next day they got out of bed and began a long climb up an unknown mountain. Their hopes were to provide a sense of normalcy for their family.

My brother lived well beyond what the doctors predicted due to my parents' tireless efforts to rise up and create their own reality. I will always be indebted to my parents for my life and for the effort they put forth to do the best they could under unthinkable circumstances with what little they had. How they managed to keep themselves collected under such stress is beyond me. They put themselves aside and did everything they could to make our lives as comfortable as possible while loving us with all their hearts.

The unspoken reality in our home was that as long as my brother lived my mother would have to sacrifice her life to ensure his survival. Over the first few years of Anthony's life my mother grew into her role quickly with trial and error as her guide. One Christmas she realized that the blinking lights on the tree caused him to have seizures, so she spent an entire day redecorating the tree because she knew how much he loved it. She kept him comfortable without causing him bedsores and got him to take his medication by crushing it up in a tablespoon of oatmeal.

She also learned to be on constant alert for the chance that something as simple as having dinner could turn into an emergency. Occasionally, my brother would choke on food and stop breathing, which would set off a chain of events that always played out about the same way. My mom would jump from her chair to Anthony's side, looking downward into his mouth. If she spotted an obstruction, she'd snatch it from his mouth and examine it. If she wasn't quick enough, his bite reflex would trigger, and he'd bite her fingers. She'd let out a controlled cry while fighting the stinging pain, pleading quietly with my brother to let go because she'd learned over time that staying calm was the only way he would release. If Anthony's airway was blocked and she couldn't see the obstruction, she'd lean him forward and begin a series of back slaps. It was usually around number five that panic would set in, and she'd yell, "Come on Anthony!" Then she'd move directly in front of him where I could see her perfectly as she pressed her thumbs into the base of his throat to trigger his gag reflex. While I watched my mother fight to clear Anthony's airway, I would remain motionless, holding my own breath as I waited to see what would happen.

My peripheral vision would start to blur, and it would appear as if I were watching a movie about my mom. Then a ringing in my ears would develop, competing with the sound of my mother's voice yelling to my brother, "Breathe!"

My mom lived every moment in the present and never took a day off. Through her actions I defined a woman and mother as being a pillar of strength and selflessness.

My sister and I were often left home alone together, usually when my mother would rush my brother to the hospital for reasons I never knew. If it grew dark, I'd get on my pajamas, brush my teeth, and Anne would be the one to put me to bed. At times my parents would return home after I was in bed and, no longer able to withstand the strain of their circumstances, they would argue. If I woke up to the sound of my parents' loud voices, I'd slip out of bed and run to my sister's room and get into her bed. She'd cover my ears with a pillow and hum until my parents could regain their strength.

During the day she protected me from the neighborhood bully, Andy. He was the redheaded teenager who lived across the street and took great pleasure in throwing my hat in a tree or tearing my underwear off through the back of my pants. Most days he just walked up and spit through the gap in his front teeth onto my shirt or in my face. He was older than me and bigger than me, and the only thing I could do was call out for Anne. The front door would fly open and out she'd step. The sight of Anne on our front porch was enough to send Andy on his way. Through many difficult times my sister eased my burden by taking on the weight of my challenges. I always treasured her and the times we shared, but more importantly I always loved her for nurturing me when she was only a child herself.

What Anne did for me I tried to do for Anthony. I took great pride in the fact we looked alike with dark brown hair and light brown eyes. Our noses were rounded exactly the same and our eyebrows were equally thick, but our bodies were very different. His skin was very pale and he was tiny for his age. His hands were always closed, his knees and elbows bent. He had little control over his body, so he had to remain on his back or reclined in a chair. He also drooled due to his condition, so we kept a folded paper towel tucked under his cheek, and it was my job to change it as often as I saw fit. It was also my job to make him laugh, which made him kick his legs and, if we were lucky, let out a snort that made both of us laugh. I felt a great sense of self-worth in knowing I was important in his life.

Although the relationship Anthony and I shared had great depth, I can only recall pieces. We spent a lot of time together, and we were often alone for hours at a time while my mom tended to our home. During that time I'd mimic my mom and gently open his hands and blow on his palms. I'd help him stretch his thin legs by rubbing behind his knees. Sometimes, I'd put my eye up to his so our eyelashes would touch because it made him laugh and I could see white disks floating in his pupils. Anthony's body was physically limited, but a strength from within allowed him to laugh and smile frequently. I was the one who could most easily make him laugh, which made us very close. I've spent my entire life trying to exemplify his strengths – while knowing it's entirely impossible.

Sharing a room with my brother had a lasting effect on my life. At night, I would climb into my bed and my mother would bring my brother to his. She'd change his diaper, turn on the humidifier, intercom and night lights. She would kiss him and say, "Good night, Ant." Then she would turn to me and with a kiss on the cheek say, "Good night." Most nights I would make shadow puppets on the wall for Anthony until he would laugh so hard he would start to snort. I'd whisper trying to calm him down, but my mom would hear and tell us it was time go to sleep.

As I got tired and felt my eyes begin to close, I'd hope for one thing, to sleep through the night. Most of the time I did, but sometimes I did not. On occasion, I'd wake up to a flood of light filling the room and the sound of the bedroom door hitting the wall as my mom rushed to

Anthony's bedside. She would have either heard him choking over the intercom or heard no sound at all, which could be just as worrisome. This type of disturbance would generally last about fifteen minutes, consisting of a few health checks or a thumb to the throat to clear his airway, followed by me trying to fall back asleep.

However, my bigger nighttime concern was being woken up by what I thought of as a 'flash-bang.' A flash-bang would happen after I was asleep and consisted of a flash of white light followed by a loud "bang" noise. The sudden jolt to my system would make me sit up in bed, gasping for air with a loud pitched ringing in my ears. Flash-bangs frightened me so much I would often stay awake until morning out of fear it would happen again. I attributed these episodes to a subconscious reflex brought on by my mother's midnight runs. It was a side effect of living life on high alert.

On Sunday mornings, Anne and I would get up early, eat breakfast in front of the television then get dressed by nine-thirty because we went to church. Once ready, we'd stand at the front door looking down the road watching for our Aunt Fannie's white Chevy Impala to come rolling up the road. When she turned into the driveway we'd yell goodbye to Mom, head out the door and climb into the Chevy's backseat. We then drove around the corner to pick up our Aunt Ursula. Aunt Urs, as we called her, would always get in the car and immediately begin talking about everything from the weather to her morning bowel movement with comments like, "Too much pepper in the sauce last night. I'm as loose as a goose."

Rain or shine we'd arrive fifteen minutes early for mass each week without exception, and listen to the church bells ring as we got out of the car. As we walked through the church doors, the sound of the organ would fill the air as people began shuffling in. I'd scoop holy water from a bowl next to the door onto my fingers and flick it in my face and say, "Amen."

The inside of the church was lined with stained glass windows and between each window was a station of the crucifixion of Christ. Each station was mounted on a black marble slate topped with a bronzed Jesus wearing a crown of thorns with an exposed rib cage, and in one scene, a guy was whipping him. The altar was a large stage with a twenty-foot-tall crucifix suspended from the vaulted ceiling above looking down on us. Speakers all around it piped the organ music through the church as we settled into our pews. When the mass was about to commence, the music would change and the priest would appear with a procession of young and old surrounding him as he made his way to the altar. We would sit and watch as he prepared to cast his words of wisdom upon the congregation and tell us why we should be thankful.

"All rise," he'd say, and that was our cue to begin our fifty-minute workout that consisted of standing up, sitting down and kneeling over and over. Throughout the mass, we had plenty of opportunities to sing as loud as possible along with the choir and my aunts seized every chance they got. The mass itself was structured the same way every week, and I would follow along because it was the right thing to do.

When I chose to listen, I heard an emphasis on sins and asking for forgiveness. The priest talked about the Holy Spirit and transcending into heaven if I lived a good life and going to hell if I did not. One other stipulation for getting into heaven was believing Jesus was the son of God, and that he died for our sins. I never really understood how he could have died for my sins since his life was two thousand years prior to mine. He also healed the sick, walked on water, and came back to life after dying. These basic beliefs were taught every Sunday, simple enough that a child could understand them – and perhaps that was the intention. However, for me, none of it made sense.

At the end of the mass everyone said, "Peace be with you," and we were on our way to Aunt Fannie's car, trying to beat the other cars out of the parking lot. Anne and I would watch out the back window and look at the determined faces of the drivers looking straight ahead with no intention of granting us the courtesy of letting us in. Once a driver looked our way we'd call out, "Go!" and Fannie would slowly inch her Impala back into the flow of cars. For us, it was important to get on the road as quickly as possible, so we could stop at the bakery and get a few loaves of bread on our way to my grandma's house.

Every Sunday our entire family would meet at my grandma's house for an early dinner around the time my dad came home from work. Entering my grandma's home I followed the maze of rubber carpet runners past her plastic-covered furniture on my way to the kitchen where my grandma would be standing over numerous pots on the stove, surrounded by my family. The moment I saw her, I'd call out to her, "Grandma!"

She would turn to me and raise her arms over her head and with a perfect smile she would say, "My baby!" She would then grab me by my face and begin kissing me over and over until I'd have to pull away. My mom and dad would arrive shortly after us, pushing Anthony through the door in a stroller. When he arrived, my grandma would turn down the stove, my aunts would set down their spoons and meatballs and everyone would head into the living room to greet him. Grandma would begin clapping her hands together and singing to him in Italian. The only word I understood was his name. He would get very excited and would laugh as everyone crowded around him to say hello. I stood off to the side and watched as my grandma held his face and began kissing him until I'd break it up by calling out, "Give the kid some room." I'd hear a few laughs because they thought I was jealous, and I'd play along, but the reality was I knew he couldn't escape the smothering.

Once I knew Anthony was settled, I'd head out to the backyard, which was outlined with fruit trees and filled with berry vines and my cousins. I'd watch for a moment as they ran in different directions with separate agendas, and I would figure out if they were playing a game or collecting apples and strawberries for my grandma to make pies. My uncles were usually off to the side telling stories while playing horseshoes or bocce ball. While I enjoyed the feeling of being part of a large family, usually I just sat and watched.

If my grandma's yard on Sundays was a hive of family activity, my own backyard was my special refuge, where I alone controlled the day. I recall feeling a sense of relief every time I walked out our backdoor and headed down the small hill that descended into a chain link fortified world where I felt safe and happy. I spent most of my time searching for bugs in the garden or digging tunnels in the sandbox. I also experienced the simple pleasures of lying on the grass and gazing at the clouds, watching for birds and dragonflies. Near our old metal shed was a patch of maple trees I called "The Woods." I had created a fort from old plywood and plastic sheets my dad had left behind the shed. Tucked under some leafy tree branches to hide us both, the fort opened to the front in a way that allowed me to slide all the way in and see only trees and the side of the shed. Most of my fort time I spent splitting blades of grass to make bracelets or pretending I was someone else, like Robin Hood, living deep in the forest.

I loved the fort the most when it rained, but not just because it stayed dry in a downpour. When the rain began tapping against the wood it created a soothing hypnotic space for me to curl into, and I would look out at my slice of the world through the water dripping in the doorway. I'd listen as the birds called to each other through the breeze, with the chatter of the maple leaves catching the drops of water mid-flight in the background. The old metal shed slowly transformed into a waterfall as the rain rolled off its roof. I'd look out my doorway and think how grateful I was to be alive and that's when the best part would happen.

If I was at peace and the moment was just right, the inside wall of the fort would develop a small black and white swirling image. If I didn't look directly at or away from the shape it would slowly start to expand and develop color. Then it would open up and in the center I could see images like a movie. The movies never lasted very long but they were all made up of scenes of people and places I'd never seen before. I saw dense cities with people walking down the sidewalks or cars driving along country roads. One time I saw a place where all the streets were made of water with boats traveling down them instead of cars. Sometimes people from the movie would walk up to the screen and look right at me. I remember a woman holding a child on her hip who looked into my eyes and smiled. I smiled back. That image remains vivid to this day. When I was alone in my fort, watching movies or just sitting in the rain, it seemed as if everything made sense and I felt free. It is for memories like these that I exercise my mind to remember my past in greater detail while other memories I access with more control.

Some memories from my childhood are visually and emotionally challenging and I've learned to control recalling them – although they will always be part of me. One memory I learned to control many years ago began when my parents went over to my grandmother's and left Anne and me at home with Anthony. He was already in bed and I had just finished brushing my teeth when the doorbell rang. A moment later I heard loud noises coming from the living room and then I heard Anne yell, "Stop it! Get out of here!"

In fear, I ran to my parents' room and called 911 from the phone on my mom's bedside table. A woman instantly answered and said, "This is 911."

"Someone broke into our house," I said.

Anne continued yelling, "Get off me!"

I dropped the phone and looked down the hallway. I could see two guys in my house and one was holding Anne against the wall. He had one hand holding her arm and the other on her neck. Without thinking I ran towards them down the hallway and into the kitchen. They didn't see me because they were focused on Anne, so I grabbed the metal broom from the side of the refrigerator and ran into the living room swinging the broom like a baseball bat as hard as I could at the guy holding Anne. The broom made a loud noise when it hit him in the back of the head. He let go of Anne and put his hands over his head as he ran out the door, and that's when I realized it was Andy and one of his friends. Anne slammed the door behind them and locked it the moment it shut. A minute later red and blue lights were flashing through the front windows and my parents pulled up in front of our house.

A few months later there was a quick trial, Anne had to testify, and Andy and his friend were put on probation for a year. Anne became extremely quiet after testifying. My parents explained to me that her life and circumstances were different from the way I viewed things. To me everything was simple, but Anne's situation was a bit more complicated and she needed some time to think. Months later she announced, "I'm in love, and I'm moving out."

Her decision came as a shock to all of us because she was only seventeen. My parents couldn't stop her from leaving, and I was devastated to see them powerless. I had lived with Anne my entire life, and I cherished all my time with her, especially the good times we shared. She had looked after me, protected me, comforted me, and now that was over. When she left it happened so quickly that the only thing I recall her saying to me was, "Don't put up with crap from anyone." She was older than me, smarter than me and just like that, she was gone.

A few months after my sister left, my dad took a job that would transfer us to the east end of Long Island. My mom and dad sat me down at the kitchen table and informed me that we were moving to a new town thirty minutes away and I'd be going to a new school. They said it would be a chance for us to start over, but what they really meant was it would be a chance for us to start healing the hole in our hearts. Even though the decision seemed sudden, I knew moving was for the best and looked forward to it. School was easy for me and I didn't have any close friends, plus I always felt empty when I passed Anne's room. I can't imagine how difficult it must have been for my parents to know she was gone.

Our house sold in one day and thirty days later it was empty. My parents were finishing off some last minute details in the house, and I was in the backyard saying goodbye to our garden, "The Woods," and my childhood. My dad stepped outside and could see the sadness on my face. "We're ready to go," he said, "and I want you to be the last one to leave this yard. We'll be waiting in the car." He always knew just what to say.

I was standing there staring, wondering if I'd ever see my home again, when I noticed Andy and his friend in the neighbor's yard pulling weeds from their flower garden. I walked over to the fence where he was kneeling and said, "See you around."

Without looking up, Andy said, "One less retard on the block."

I knew his comment was directed at my brother in one final effort to hurt me and all I could think of was Anne's words. I stood there breathing and the years of humiliation he'd caused me flooded through me. In that moment, I became a helpless passenger in my body as I pulled myself up on the fence, opened the zipper of my pants, and began peeing on Andy's back. The moment he realized what was happening he jumped up with surprise and said, "What the hell are you doing?"

His friend began pointing and rolled onto his back laughing.

"You're dead! I'm going to find you and you're dead!" he yelled while pulling off his shirt.

I sprinted back through the house and got quickly into the car with my parents. My heart was pumping and I was breathing heavily, but I felt liberated by what had just happened. I sat next to my brother, and he smiled as we rolled away down our road, knowing we were leaving this part of our lives behind us and stepping into an unknown future.

Whether life takes the form of a human, a dragonfly, or a green blade of grass, each will be further defined by its environment and the information contained within it. We come into this world in a unique situation that begins to shape who we are and who we'll become. The moment we understand what we accept as reality has been created through specific places, relationships and events, we are no longer entirely at the mercy of our circumstances and can begin to alter our lives and future through our actions.

II

EXPERIENCE

We are just a whisper in the eye of a hurricane.

It is through our interaction with all things that our life can maintain an anchor in this world. Experience makes us participants in the creation of reality, and our minds associate seemingly independent events allowing us to define our beliefs. Without this ability, the world around us would be a prison of chaotic moments and random noise. Experience defines our freedom and our fears.

The process of using our senses to experience events allows us to identify patterns providing a reality we can trust. *Experience is the catalyst to our growth, and it ignites our existence.* As I continued to grow, my experiences accelerated my understanding of life and further defined who I would become.

I believe autumn is the time for new beginnings. It's just a feeling I get that causes a reaction within my mind, and I begin to reflect on my life for a period of time. This belief may have developed from years of sensory stimulation caused by watching the trees change color and listening to the sound of a cool breeze as it washed over the drying leaves. Or, it could have come from the social conditioning of the school year starting in the fall, bringing with it new challenges and new faces. Regardless of which is true, the cycle of events during this season ingrained in me the desire to continually reevaluate my life, make changes and create new beginnings.

The earliest I recall trying to make some sense of the world around me was when we moved to the northeast shore of Long Island to a town called Shoreham in the fall of 1981. As we drove to our new house I noticed the roads were narrow and winding, with dips and turns that caused my stomach to leap. Our neighborhood was tucked into a small forest, and our house was set between several large, vine-draped trees. Across the street, an open field of patchy grass surrounded by a chain link fence was marked with a sign that read "Town Park." That park was backed by miles of undeveloped land serving as a buffer to a nuclear power plant under construction on the local beach.

Our new house was different and brought with it some major changes. My brother and I no longer shared a room. My dad was suddenly around and more available to me, and my mother graduated from the school of hard knocks with a diploma in caring for Anthony, who had already survived far beyond medical predictions. She was finally afforded the luxury of a little free time. I was granted independence in the form of my own space where I began to shape my world to be as comfortable and consistent as possible. I replaced nightlights with moonlight and the sound of a humidifier with music from a new stereo. I no longer had to hide to be alone, which allowed me the freedom to relax and think about my life. I also spent a lot of time exploring in the woods behind the park, walking the paths and climbing on boulders the size of my house, experiencing the sense of peace that came with sitting on a fallen tree. At moments while walking through the woods I'd look up at the canopy of leaves and watch particles of dust glitter in streams of sunlight and, no longer able to hold back my happiness, I'd begin to cry.

It was at this time in my life that I began to create a richer view of the world around me. At the beginning of seventh grade in my new school, my placement test results showed I was at a fourth-grade reading level and was placed in remedial classes. While I now understood why I'd found my old school so effortless, it made me angry. All of my new classmates were way ahead of me simply because of where they happened to live, and it wasn't fair. Over time my anger turned to gratitude for the teachers at my new school who took the time to work with me and got me caught up quickly.

A few weeks into the start of classes, a kid invited me to join him and his friends for lunch. But when I walked up, they were all quiet and none of them said a word. Then a blond-haired boy pushed me backwards, and as I stumbled, I grabbed his shirt and pulled him with me, and we began to struggle. A punch to my mouth made the other boys begin to cheer, which increased my adrenaline and my heart began to race. In an instant, I made the choice to fight back, which would further define who I was to become. Over the course of the next thirty seconds, the two of us punched and pulled at each other while the other boys watched and yelled. Then as quickly as it had started, it stopped. A teacher grabbed both of us by our arms, pulled us apart, and told the other boys to go sit down. The teacher pointed at me and said, "You go to the nurse, and Jake, go to the office." At the teacher's words, I glanced down at my shirt and noticed it was covered with blood. He handed me a napkin from his pocket and told me to put pressure on my lip to stop the bleeding, and my body began to shake uncontrollably as I left the room and walked down the hallway. The nurse greeted me and examined my lip then wiped the blood from my face with a wet towel. She handed me a bag of ice then walked me to the office, where I sat on a bench next to Jake. We sat quietly for a moment until I lowered the bag of ice from my mouth and looked at him.

"I'm sorry," he said.

I held out my hand, looked him in the eye, and replied, "I'm Frank."

That event resulted in five stitches to my top lip and a friendship with Jake that would last for many years. The experience we shared bonded us at a level of respect that can't be attained through a simple verbal exchange. I don't recommend making friends in this fashion but it worked for us. Sharing a powerful experience with another person creates a bond that makes everything related to them more meaningful.

My brother was also exposed to new experiences with our move, particularly when he began to go to school for the first time, marking a couple of milestones for our family. The school required him to take a bus and the bus required him to have a wheelchair. My mom applied to be the aide on his bus, and she got her first paying job in twenty years doing what she knew best. The day his wheelchair arrived at our house my mother inspected it thoroughly then strapped Anthony in and started making a series of minor adjustments while my brother stared at her face with a smile.

When my mom felt confident that he was secured properly she rolled him slowly down the hallway and back, and I couldn't help notice that she looked concerned. But my focus quickly shifted to the fact that my brother was now on wheels and it was time to introduce him to a new experience. My mom stepped aside and I walked up behind his chair and grabbed the handles. We started out slowly, going through the kitchen, but when we entered our long hallway I made a screeching noise and began running as fast as I could down the hallway. I was making engine noises and Anthony was laughing and snorting at the same time. When we reached the end of the hallway I made another screeching noise before spinning him around and racing back. I couldn't see his face, but I could certainly hear his laughter and I could feel his legs kicking with every step I took. After a few runs, my mom began to smile and clap her hands. As we raced past her, she called out, "Hold on Ant! You're going brooom brooom!"

Mom no longer looked concerned but relieved. She confided in me later that night that when she fastened him into the wheelchair it felt as if she was giving up on him ever walking, but when he raced by with such excitement she saw his new freedom. It was moments like this where I had the advantage of not constantly being concerned about my brother's well-being, instead just enjoying being his brother. All three of us played a part in the creation of that experience, and it connected us at a moment in time. That moment taught me that trusting my instincts allows me to be my best and create unforgettable moments regardless of the circumstances.

Shortly after my thirteenth birthday we took our first family trip to Florida to visit my grandmother who had moved to a mobile home park with my aunts the prior year, taking with them Sunday dinners, church and the love of a grandmother. My mom spent many days preparing for the trip by creating checklists, packing bags and filling prescriptions to ensure that no item would be left behind. When the day came, our station wagon was neatly packed with nearly every bit of clothing we owned and everything needed to keep my brother comfortable on a three-day car trip.

The plan was to stay with my Aunt Urs for up to four weeks while my mom and dad spent time with my grandmother in the hospital where she was being treated for advanced stages of colon cancer. It seemed like a simple plan to me, and I was looking forward to seeing her. What I didn't realize at the time was that this trip would be measured not in distance but in depth of experience.

We drove eleven hours that first day and stayed at a roadside motel off Interstate 95 in Fayetteville, North Carolina. The accommodations were cramped. We shared a single room with two beds, and Anthony was on a rollaway cot surrounded by unpacked pill bottles, diapers, drinking cups, pillows, and blankets. My mom had planned for every contingency since it was his first night away from home that was not in a hospital.

I remember that night vividly because I fell asleep early, and I awoke to a flash-bang. My first thought was hard to hold because of the loud ringing in my ears, but it was one of surprise since this was the first flash-bang I'd experienced since we moved to our new house, and it lasted longer than the ones I remembered from the past. My body was humming,

31

my heart was pounding hard in my chest, and I was having trouble catching my breath. After a few moments, I struggled to open my eyes and when I did, I was looking down into the hotel room, able to see everything from above – including myself in bed and my brother on his rollaway cot. In confusion and fear I closed my eyes and when I opened them I was back in my motel bed as the ringing slowly faded away. I would spend the rest of the night fighting the stinging in my eyes to keep them open so I could stay awake until morning.

The next day we packed up the car and got back on the road and I slept in the backseat to make up for the night before. My brother, on the other hand, did not fall asleep once in the car for the entire trip. He kept his eyes open, looking out the window with a smile as the landscape alongside the highway passed him by.

After three days and fourteen-hundred miles, our dust-covered green station wagon came to rest in front of my Aunt Ursula's mobile home. We were greeted by aunts, uncles, cousins and the smell of sulfur in the hot humid air. My mom immediately rushed my brother into the air conditioned mobile home where she spent the next two hours converting my aunt's trailer into our temporary home. After we were settled in, my parents left to visit my grandmother who was lying in a hospital bed weighing just a fraction of what she had before. The days began to pass, and I would hear reports of her bravery in the face of death as I sat in the air-conditioned trailer on a plastic-covered sofa bed next to my brother watching a thirteen-inch black-and-white TV with a coat hanger for an antenna. The days were long and the hours dragged on slowly due to lack of stimulation. At that point in my life, moments of interest defined who I was and the rest of the time I was just waiting for something new to happen.

Three weeks after we moved into my aunt's trailer, my grandmother convinced the doctors that they couldn't do anything more for her, and she was going to leave to be home with her family, since they had all come to town to see her. My dad and Aunt Fanny brought her home and put her in her bed, and my mom began to shuttle between the two trailers taking care of Anthony and taking care of my grandma. The next day I watched from across the street as a procession of family members entered and left her trailer, some crying, others serious, but no one ever left with a smile. That night I asked when I would get to see her and my dad explained to me that it would be too difficult with her in this condition, but he was soon overruled by a higher power.

Early the next morning my dad came into our trailer and told me my grandmother insisted on seeing me, but she was very sick and I might not recognize her. I tried to prepare myself as I crossed the street by imagining how different she might look. When I was led into her room, the moment I saw her all I could see was my grandma with her arms stretched out to give me a hug. I walked over to her and we hugged while my dad held onto my shirt to make sure I didn't lean on her too much. As I moved back, I could see she was thin and frail and her skin was a little yellow, but she still looked like my grandmother. She began to open her mouth to speak, and I saw that her teeth were brown and several were missing. It was at that moment our eyes met, and she quickly closed her mouth and began gesturing to a glass on the bedside table that contained her teeth. Unfortunately I was the only one in the room who knew what she wanted, and my dad quickly walked me out of her room before I could say anything. As I left, I looked back to see my grandmother for the last time smiling with her lips pressed together and her eyes looking directly into mine.

Back at my aunt's trailer my Dad asked me if I was okay then headed back to be with his mother. I sat on the couch next to my brother and tried to process what I had just experienced. When I finally looked at the black-and-white TV, I saw the president of the United States surrounded by people with the newscaster repeating, "President Reagan has been shot!" as the footage replayed before my eyes. My dying grandmother and the image of the president being shot are now fused together in my mind and I cannot think of one without the other. That experience made me realize life is extremely fragile and limited.

My grandmother died the Wednesday after we returned home. The following morning my dad was standing holding a suitcase by our front door talking with my mother. The only sentence I remember him saying was, "I'm an orphan." That simple statement made me realize how experiences outside of myself that were important to me could also be significant to others in different ways. For the first time, I began to wonder what it was like to be someone else.

Experiences are never independent, but always part of a cause and effect relationship. An experience is born when we chose to participate in creating something new. Our contributions to an experience helps shape our reality and offers us a connection to others. Sometimes a chain reaction of events occurs when one decision or experience triggers unanticipated new experiences. The relationship between the planned and unplanned experience shapes what we call, 'our path'.

As we grow older, those sorts of paths start to emerge more clearly. My teenage years were exceptionally valuable in defining my path since during that period I experienced many memorable firsts. My first job for instance was as an aide on a bus transporting handicapped children to school. Since I was already uniquely trained for that line of work I jumped at the opportunity when my mom told me about it. It turned out that the children I was transporting were not children at all.

Jimmy was twenty-one with cerebral palsy and wore plastic molds on his arms because he had a tendency to bite himself until he would bleed. Sofia was fifteen, mildly retarded, and blind because her stepfather put pennies under her eyelids as a form of punishment. And Paul, who also had cerebral palsy, wore a helmet to protect him since he was prone to severe seizures. He liked to yell really loud, had a full beard, and was much bigger than me.

Like anyone, it took me a few days to get comfortable with my new job. I was extremely nervous the first time Debbie the bus driver showed me how to lock the wheelchairs in place and I quickly realized the safety of these people was in my hands. The wheels of their wheelchairs needed to roll between two brackets mounted on the floor so I could slide a metal safety rod between the spokes to keep them from rolling. Then I would lock the rods in place with wing nuts that I would hand tighten until my fingers began to sting.

After a week I became more comfortable in my new role, and I would try to entertain everyone on the thirty-minute ride. Sometimes Jimmy would put his plastic covered arm on Paul's tray, and I would say "Hey, you can't do that." Then I'd unbuckle my belt to get up and Jimmy would quickly pull his arm back causing an eruption of laughter from everyone. It was a game we played and all enjoyed. We also created a radio game when the stations tuned in and out of reception while our yellow mini bus traveled its way across the island past sod farms and potato fields. I'd cheer when the music came on and Paul would stomp his feet and laugh with excitement, and Sofia would hold her arms up and swing from side to side humming. One time Jimmy decided to play the arm game as we were waiting for the music to return then I saw Paul, his eyes rolled back and his head thrust forward. In the absence of music the only sound heard was the crack of plastic as I watched Paul's face landing on Jimmy's cast. I jumped from my seat and lifted Paul's head but it was too late to save him from injuring himself. A thick stream of blood hung from his mouth and nose and the breeze from the open window blew bits of it free and onto my shirt. In that moment I felt paralyzed while I held Paul's head as his seizure slowly subsided.

I couldn't speak when Debbie called out, "Do I need to stop?!" Suddenly, the radio reception returned and Sofia cheered and swayed back and forth with her arms bent up into the air. As Paul's seizure ended, I slowly regained my ability to move and carefully started to clean the blood from his face with paper towels. Jimmy was fine but that was the end of the arm game. That first job brought with it experiences involving taking care of others. It also sparked other experiences, creating a chain reaction that influenced my life.

Debbie's husband was a disk jockey at a local radio station and on any given day she'd bring me a new album to critique. This chance connection gave me the opportunity to be exposed to a vast diversity of music as a teenager that I wouldn't have heard otherwise. The most memorable album she ever handed me had a black and white cover with a picture of two of the musicians leaning on each other.

I took that album home and in the quiet of my room I put the needle down and with a few pops, Bruce Springsteen's music filled my room for the first time and I began to make a new connection. His music communicated to me in a way that I understood with great clarity and emotion. I listened to that album exclusively for the next few weeks until I could close my eyes and visualize every story – resulting in a connection to someone I had not met through their creation.

This first job also brought what I would consider the most important event of my life to that point. I was able to save enough money to buy a charcoal gray '76 Camaro and with that purchase found a freedom I had never imagined. I would drive from shore to shore listening to Springsteen with my new girlfriend in the passenger seat holding my hand. When I wasn't driving my car, Jake and I would spend endless hours taking it apart to understand how it worked. This string of experiences made me feel alive and independent for the first time and opened up new paths for me to explore.

In the fall of my senior year, for a period of time, I really believed I had a firm grasp on life. Each day unfolded the same way with my mother and brother enjoying our breakfast routine, then off to school where I'd spend time with friends and teachers focusing on our tight-knit community. The days were simple and predictable until mother nature changed our plans. Events began to unfold above the Atlantic Ocean that eventually forced their way into our lives.

A storm was beginning to form off the coast of Florida with intense winds and heavy rain. At night I lay in bed soaking up music from my stereo while the cool breeze filled my room with fresh evening air. Over the Atlantic, the winds picked up and the storm absorbed the ocean, while starting to swirl. Even as I got up the next morning and followed my daily routine, the storm did the same. After several days and hundreds of miles between us, the storm that began from nothing opened its eye and hurricane Gloria was born.

Gloria became the main topic of conversation from school to the dinner table to the corner market. Everyone knew the facts about Gloria, and we shared them and our views about her as a community. Her description was ever changing, from her whereabouts and strength to her direction and potential for destruction. She brought people together and called us to action. She moved up the coast and headed directly toward us as batteries and water began to disappear from the shelves of stores with boarded-up windows. After several days of anticipation, it was finally determined that Gloria had her eye set on our small town of Shoreham.

For most people, the anticipation of the storm's arrival was a time to joke with kids excited about the schools being closed, but only one conversation existed in our house, and it wasn't funny. If we lost power for a long period of time how would we care for my brother? My dad bought a generator and enough fuel to last a month while my mom stocked the house with food and prescriptions. We were as ready as we could possibly be. The hurricane made land on a Tuesday and within minutes the power went out. With the sound of the pounding wind and rain in the background, my mother said defiantly, "Alright, here we go!"

Standing at the window watching the wind twist and bend the world before my eyes was an amazing experience. Buckets of rain fell from the darkened sky and slammed into our house while gusts of wind blew debris down our street. The pounding on our roof was so loud we had to yell inside the house to hear each other. The storm pounded our house for more than hour – then suddenly stopped, the sun coming out. My dad

40

called me to the back door, and we walked outside. He pointed to the sky and said, "This is the eye of the hurricane. Few people have ever stood where we're standing right now. Here it's calm while there's a storm raging in every direction."

We stood in the stillness of that moment and listened. The only sounds we heard were drops of water until a few minutes later a rumbling sound began off in the distance, and I could see a black line of clouds approaching. My dad said, "That's the back wall of the eye. The most dangerous part of the storm."

"Why is that?" I asked.

"Because the wind has weakened everything around us, and now it'll switch direction and come around again." He was right. During the second half of the hurricane, trees snapped and were suspended in the air for a moment before slamming to the ground. Branches blew down the road, trash and debris piled in the streets and against houses. When it was over, we had lost seven trees, our screened porch, hot water, and power for five days.

Each of those nights before the power returned, I would lie in the dark listening to the hum of our generator and wonder how I could have been so lucky to stand in the eye of a hurricane. Decisions made by others may affect me directly, but I become further defined by how I react to events that are for the most part out of my control. Months after the storm had passed, another type of storm had begun to form in the events of my own personal life. In what was seeming to become a common practice, my parents sat me down and informed me that my dad had taken a job on an exciting new project, and we would be moving to Florida. I'd be able to finish high school in New York, but any thoughts of college would have to wait until after we moved. In an instant my girlfriend, my friends, and my confidence about the future were replaced by disappointment and frustration. Without a word, I walked out the door, got in my car, and started driving across town to my girlfriend's house. Along the way, I began to think, "Why now? Not now." I was determined to find a way to stay and keep my friends and girlfriend and my life intact. I began to think of friends I could stay with and ways I could earn money.

As I became focused on what I needed to do, I looked down and pressed play on my Springsteen tape. When I looked up all I could see was the grill of a truck as it plowed into my driver's side door. The car spun backwards and all I could hear was the sound of snapping wood and glass falling until it was interrupted by the sound of a tremendous blow to the back of my head. My car had spun through a post and rail fence and one of the rails had speared through the rear window, striking the back of my head

42

and snapping it forward before breaking through the front windshield, harpooning the car.

The moment the car was still, barely conscious, I attempted to open my door, but it was crushed. I turned to get out the passenger side door and was met again by the rail this time square in my forehead. I could not process what was happening, only aware that I was trapped. My window had been shattered, so I desperately wiggled my way out over the broken glass, landing on the grass of the yard I had just spun through. I stumbled to the street and saw the truck with its front end crushed and the driver standing with his hands clasped on top of his head. I immediately scanned the intersection for a clue of what had happened and noticed a stop sign from the back that I hadn't seen from the front.

My head was throbbing and I began to stumble down the street when a man appeared holding his hands up. "Please. Please," he said. "You need to sit down. Just sit right there and please don't move."

That's when I remembered the rail and felt the back of my head, which was wet. I tilted my head downward and held my hand out into a stream of blood that overflowed my hand onto the street. The instant I sat down, two people held me steady by the arms while another person applied pressure to my head with the shirt off his back. It was when someone yelled, "Call an ambulance!" that I realized I was in the care of complete strangers, and I struggled to stay awake until the ambulance arrived.

After stitches and x-rays, I was released from the hospital and sat at home with bandages around my head and a soon-to-be hockey stick shaped scar on the back of my head. A part of me felt as though I had been through something life-changing. I'd survived a crushing blow to my head and walked away with only stitches. I felt lucky that I had survived, but petrified that I could have died in an instant. That thought kept me from leaving the house, and I sat at home and looked out the window for days, not wanting to go anywhere or talk with anyone. I spent those days lost in my mind, trying to make sense of what had happened. Everything was great one moment; the next, my car was gone and I was thinking about dying. A single experience can change everything without notice.

After a week of sitting at home, Jake came by on his way to the junkyard to look for a radiator cap and asked me to come along. I agreed to go and the drive actually began to make me feel better. At the junkyard, surrounded by the smell of old engine oil dripping from cracked crankcases, we began climbing in and out of the wrecks, popping hoods looking for the right cap. Jake tapped me on the shoulder and pointed at a Camaro with a crushed front end and said, "There's your new car."

I stared at it for a moment and I began to smile. The thought of building a car out of two wrecks felt right. It pulled me from my fear of the recent past and into the reality of the world that I knew with a friend I could trust. The entire ride home we talked about strategy and how we would tackle each detail of building this car. The conversation felt safe and comfortable. I was beginning a restoration process for myself – and my car – with a very close friend right by my side. When we returned to my house, he told me about a party on the beach that evening, saying he would pick me up on his way. But by the time he arrived to pick me up I had withdrawn again, deciding one outing for the day was enough. I wasn't ready to go out so shortly after my accident. He made me promise to call him in the morning so we could return to the junkyard and take another look at the car.

I was unable keep that promise. At two a.m. the following morning, the phone rang. My mom answered the phone and immediately handed it to me. It was my friend Terry speaking in a tone I barely recognized. He sounded terrified.

The only words I heard were, "Jake's dead. He's dead." Jake had run a stop sign leaving the beach party and his car had been crushed from the passenger door to the driver's seat. He had died instantly.

On hearing those words, my brain began to perform a function I had never experienced. Reality began to flicker in my mind. I heard the words that Jake was dead, but my mind only accepted it as reality in sporadic cycles. I would experience tremendous anguish followed by shock and disbelief. The moments I believed he was truly gone were so painful and confusing that my consciousness would shift back to where somehow he was alive which, although unrealistic, gave me a brief reprieve from suffering. The reality of his death was just too difficult for me to accept all at once.

The next few days I remember as if those moments were burned into my heart. I had my close friends, events to busy my mind, but I still felt weak and alone. With every silent moment or any pause in conversation, I would think about Jake. I had never known this kind of searing pain and emotional aguish. Through it all, my one constant thought was that I was going to have to deal with it because it was now a part of me.

At Jake's funeral, it seemed like the entire town had come to pay their respects. Standing before them, I was holding onto the handle of my friend's casket with my mouth quivering and tears in my eyes. As I talked to as many people as I could to silence my own thoughts, I began to realize just how many people he knew, and how many different types of relationships he developed impacting his own life. A hole had been torn in the fabric of our community as well as my heart.

A few weeks after Jake's funeral I received a check in the mail from my insurance company to cover the cost of damages to my car. That check gave me just enough money to buy the wreck in the junkyard and a challenge to occupy my mind. The following week a flatbed tow truck delivered the car and I began to labor night after night to join the two wrecks together. Over the next few months I steadied my mind while listening to Springsteen and circling the wrecks in search of myself. Two months and five days later, I got in that car, started the engine and began to follow the taillights of my parents' car onto the highway heading south. I couldn't help but wonder as I stepped on the accelerator if I was heading for a new beginning or if I was in the eye of a storm heading for the back wall.

We experience therefore we exist. Reality is a constant chain reaction of events and life plays a significant role in their creation through the experience. Seemingly infinite numbers of events have been swirling since the beginning of time but we can only experience the events we are exposed to. Events of the past are history and events of the present are experience. As we experience in the present we continually define what we believe to be real, shaping our future choices and defining our understanding of the world.

III

TIME

Death is a stone cast into the calm waters of mortality.

Time is our only true possession. We spend every moment trying to hold on to it, afraid to look back, and blind to where it's taking us. It is the common denominator that we share with all things, and it sets the stage for our life and allows existence. Time will give us everything and will eventually take it all away.

We exist within time and the speed at which we pass through it depends on our current situation. For example, if we're in a less than pleasant situation, such as waiting for a bus in freezing rain, then time seems to move excruciatingly slow where every minute feels like five. It will also continue to slow incrementally as the situation gets worse such as if the bus is late. The opposite is also true. If we are reading an interesting book, then an hour may seem like ten minutes. The better the book, the faster time will pass. It appears the more conscious we are of time the slower it moves but that's not always true. The older we get we become more conscious of how quickly time passes. *Time is a means to measure*

Understanding. With our move to Florida I became more aware of the inconsistency of time.

When I arrived in Florida, I felt an instant disconnect from everything around me, including my parents. The air was hot and humid and smelled like sulfur. After two days, I developed a painful sinus infection that lasted for weeks and recurred regularly. My parents' house was under new construction in a developing community with four bedrooms and a pool. As nice as it was I somehow felt like an uninvited guest tagging along on their adventure. I developed a routine almost immediately in an effort to deal with my new situation. Each morning I got up and went to the local community college. I came home in the afternoon, slept for two hours, and then worked all night washing dishes at a nearby restaurant.

Unfortunately, I also developed a routine every night that consisted of going to bed around midnight, staring at the ceiling, struggling to breathe through my nose, and wondering how everything went wrong. I would think about how my life had changed so dramatically in a short period of time, and I would struggle with why my friend died and I lived. The nights dragged on as if time were slowing to a halt and only ended when sunlight began to fill the room, and I'd fall asleep. Sleeping in the afternoon allowed me enough rest to be able to function early mornings and late evenings when I needed to, but it also brought with it an interesting experience that would eventually help me cope.

When I'd return from class, I'd lie down on the floor of my room next to my stereo so I could listen to music with my headphones on. Within a few minutes I would begin to have vivid dreams of places I've never seen, and I would talk with people I'd never met. The memories I had of these dreams were as real as the memories I create when awake, with one exception: I was happy. After several months of this routine, I had a dream that I was sailing on a lake under a cloud-filled sky, and in the background I could hear the same music that was playing in my headphones, and I became aware that I was dreaming. It only lasted for a moment but in that moment I just sailed with the wind in my face, listening to music, and I was at peace. It wasn't long before I learned how to recreate that experience through the use of familiar music. In closing my eyes and dreaming I was able to find a way to deal with my sadness. The scenery was amazing and the people were beautiful and always happy to see me. One day I'd walk through a city, the next I'd be standing in the middle of a knee-high field of grass looking up at a blue sky. When I felt a breeze pass over, I'd look around and see it create ripples in the grass, and the sky would shimmer as if I were looking up into a crystal blue lake.

My mind had created a controlled yet intangible world in an effort to help me cope with the world of reality I faced every day, one of isolation and emotional pain. Each day was the same - I'd work, stay up all night, ignore my parents' questioning of my actions, go to school in the morning, and dream all afternoon. I saw it as an innocent escape but what happened next I would never have imagined.

One afternoon I awoke in a dream and in front of me were multi-colored trains moving slowly towards a train depot. I put my hands in my jacket pockets and walked towards the trains stepping over the tracks heading for the large building that the trains were pulling into. When I walked in I spotted a control room at the top of the building that looked down over the train yard, and I headed up the stairs to get a better view. In the train yard, all the cars were separating and changing tracks and then reconnecting. It didn't appear to be random, and I asked myself, "What's controlling all of this?"

I heard a familiar voice from behind me say, "I do."

I turned and saw Jake standing by the doorway, smiling. "Each car represents a different life, and my job is to connect them together."

Overwhelmed with emotion I said, "It's you," and with each of my teardrops his face faded until I woke up on the floor with my body shaking and my mind numb. This was the first of several times I would see Jake while dreaming, and each time I could stay focused longer, and I managed to carry on a longer conversation with him. Sometimes I would see him in a crowd but almost always he arrived as a voice from behind me.

"Hey, man, how's Florida?" he'd say.

"Good. Do you know you're dead?" I'd say.

"Yes."

"Can you tell me what it's like?"

"All I can tell you is, it's cool, and I'm happy," he would respond, and that was usually it.

If I pushed the line of questioning too much he'd turn the corner of his mouth up and smile, then tell me it was time to go.

Through these experiences, I started to feel like I was regaining control of my life. Time began to pass more quickly as my mind was finally focused on the present and less on the past. My parents didn't see it the same way. I was on the couch in our living room late one night watching TV and my mom and dad came in from their room and began to question me about what I was doing with my life.

"Do you realize that you sleep all day? And you don't talk," my mother said.

"I'm not sleeping."

"You're either on drugs or depressed. Whatever it is, you need to pay us rent starting now," my dad said, and that's when the conversation turned into an argument that ended with him saying, "If you don't like it here, leave."

That ultimatum was a challenge I hadn't expected when they walked into the room, but I agreed. I can't remember my words when I returned a week later to get my clothes, but I do recall the look on my mother's face, and it was one of disbelief.

I found a cheap one-bedroom apartment next to the railroad tracks in Melbourne. I was living on a dishwasher's salary which, after rent left barely enough money for food and none for air conditioning. I found a couch and a lamp for ten dollars at a garage sale and the guy was nice enough to help me move it. When he saw the inside of my empty apartment he told me to keep the ten dollars. My routine stayed the same but the lucid dreams began to slow because my apartment was too hot for me to sleep during the day, and eventually my dreams were replaced by paralysis.

I would lie on my back unable to move for hours, staring at the ceiling or looking around the room. Then I would wake up on the couch only to realize I was dreaming. This experience happened over and over again; I'd get caught in a loop and that was my dream. The only way for me to break the loop was to scream until I began moaning in my sleep. The sound of myself moaning was the only way I could wake up for good.

At night, if I was lucky, I'd fall asleep on the couch from exhaustion. Otherwise, I'd just lie there in the early morning hours listening to the trains rumbling past, along with the voice in my head analyzing my past decisions. The only clear awareness of time I had at that point was night and day. Time had slowed to a near standstill where minutes felt like hours and the nights would never end. Repeating the same thoughts over and over in my mind was having a direct impact on my perception of time. Without new thoughts my mind was being crushed under the weight of time and I was about to break.

One night as I lay sweating on my couch I struggled to understand how my life had dissolved before my eyes in such a short period of time. The feeling of being a caged animal whelmed up in me as the sweat from my head stung my eyes and dripped into my ringing ears. It was the dripping sound that finally put me over the edge. I jumped up from the couch and ran out the door, gasping for air. No shoes, no shirt, just a pair of gold shorts and rage in my head. I ran out of my complex and onto the road that led away from my apartment. I began sprinting and I could feel my lungs begin to heave as I picked up speed and my legs began to loosen and a pounding in the side of my head beat like a drum.

Slowly, my rage gave way to exhaustion and eventually my legs gave way to the road. I fell palms down and chest out as I slid to a halt on the pavement. The sting of hitting the ground woke me from my rage. I was down and as low as I'd ever been – literally and emotionally. I pushed myself up to my knees on the side of the road in the middle of the night, finding a little strength in the darkness. With that strength I asked for a sign.

"Please show me a sign that I'm not alone," I called out. I wasn't hoping for much. I would have taken an animal noise or a cool breeze but I saw and heard nothing – no shooting star, not even a dog bark. I was broken - a caged animal with nowhere to run.

I cried out loud for a bit with my face in my hands then attempted to stand. It was only then that I realized I had run through some broken glass and was bleeding. I took inventory of my body, finding blood mixed with dirt all over my legs. My left foot had a few cuts, but a chunk of glass was sticking out of the side of my right foot. I pulled the glass out, which released more blood from the gash in my foot, and it was at that moment I realized I had run more than a mile from my apartment.

I began the long hobble back. Beaten and alone I kept moving toward the dim light of a convenience store I had run past earlier. As I crossed the parking lot of the store, I heard the pay phone begin to ring. It was roughly three a.m., and no one was around, so I answered it. The voice of a young woman asked, "Is Greg there?"

"Greg who?" I asked.

She said, "My boyfriend. I was supposed to call him at this number now."

"There's no one here but me. Why are you calling so late?" I asked.

"He wanted me to call him and my parents don't want me talking with him anymore," she said.

"Why don't your parents want you talking with him?"

"Because he's not real nice." Her words became sharp, and she said, "He said if I didn't call him, he'd bang on my front door and wake up my dad then kick his ass." With that I could see headlights coming down the road.

"Does he drive a pickup?" I asked.

"Yes."

The pickup slid to a stop in the parking lot, and Greg got out with his finger pointing in my direction, yelling, "Are you talking to my girlfriend, bitch?" Greg was a bully.

"Hold on a minute," I said into the phone. I let the phone hang and just stood there for a moment with my bare chest, hands and face covered in a mixture of blood, sweat and dirt. Then I waved for him to come over. "Why don't you come closer to the phone so she can hear you scream while I kick your ass?" I said. Greg didn't say anything, just stared at me for a minute then got back in his truck and sped back down the road. Perhaps he knew it was over between them, or my words combined with my physical appearance affected him. I sat down next to the phone and I said, "You still there?"

"Yeah…"

"I don't think you need to worry about Greg coming to your house tonight."

"Thank you."

We talked for hours. I told her about my situation and she told me about her parents and Greg. The hours passed in what seemed like minutes, and before I knew it, there were black clouds on a blue sky as the sun began to rise. Cars began to drive by on the road in front of me, and in the distance I could see my apartment complex with a train passing in the background. When we ended the call I told her I'd stop by her work to say hello, and that I would see my parents that day and smooth things over and she said she would do the same with her parents. I spoke with her months later, and she thanked me and said Greg was out of her life. I thanked her for listening when I needed it the most. We shared that moment and went on with our lives.

If there is something that transcends this world, I had gotten my first glimpse into what it was. I had asked for a sign that I was not alone and for a few hours I was not. The experience could be written off as just a coincidence, but I didn't believe that. Instead, I believed at last that something was listening, so I started talking. Over the next year, I began to speak or, one might call it, talk to myself. It wasn't anything formal but it did allow me to articulate what was going on in my head. Sometimes I wondered if I had the start of a mental disorder. I spent a lot of time alone that year talking through my thoughts and eventually believed I was given a gift in the form of a connection to something greater than myself. That connection gave me the strength to develop a positive attitude about myself, and my situation.

Time for me had become erratic over the course of the first two years of living in Florida. In my pain and confusion it had slowed dramatically but began to accelerate again once my mind cleared those hurdles. This realization allowed me to identify when I began to mentally or emotionally falter. The speed at which time appeared to pass had become my compass guiding me out of the darkness of night and into the light of a new day.

My parents and I started talking again when my mom invited me for Thanksgiving. My mom was an amazing cook and would spend hours in the kitchen preparing for dinner. When it was time to eat, she would call us into the dining room, and we'd gather around the table while my mom propped Anthony up at the table in a high chair next to her. My brother would eat first while we would all take turns asking, "How's it going Anthony?" and "Are you excited about (fill in the holiday)?"

After Anthony had finished eating my mom would move him from the table and get him comfortable on the couch nearby where he would call out quietly in the background trying to form words with each exhale. His voice was constant and it stroked at our focus. When he wasn't calling out it was because he was struggling to breathe. Shortly after moving to Florida his breathing had worsened, and it was particularly bad in the mornings going from lying down to sitting up. Still, my mom did everything she could to include him and create some sense of normalcy. It was a constant challenge for all of us to hold it together, but we did and we did it for him as well as for ourselves.

We all acknowledged that the condition of Anthony's body did not represent the condition of his mind, but to what degree no one knew. If we believed his mind was the same as ours he would then appear to us as trapped in his body and we would be obligated to find a way to set him free. Because that belief would create an exhausting reality, trapping all of us, we chose to look past his physical body and embrace the fact that he was in there.

Anthony started slipping out of consciousness a few weeks before Christmas and my parents had to make the brutal decision not to bring him to the hospital because they knew there was nothing further they could do except the suffering. At last he fell unconscious for an entire week, which seemed like an eternity. Every night I'd stop by the house on my way home from work and sit by his bedside and watch him breathe until I felt tired. Then I'd head home, or sometimes fall asleep in my old room. It was a hard time for everyone but most importantly him. One night I had to work late so I stopped by the house but went straight to my old room to sleep and it was that night Anthony left us.

I awoke to the sound of my mother's howling with grief and pain.

That was how word of my brother's death was delivered to me. My mother sobbed uncontrollably for about an hour then began to execute the long checklist that I'm sure she had compiled in her head over many years. My father cried once for maybe a minute and stopped himself. After that he had himself collected, and I never saw him slip again. To him life and death go hand in hand - this was just part of the process.

Before the paramedics arrived, I sat with Anthony for some time. He was still and his skin was yellow. When I looked at him, I knew something was missing. It seemed that all things associated with his life had disappeared at the moment of his death. In the blink of an eye, it was all gone. He was gone, and I could see it with my eyes.

In the company of the police, a Catholic priest arrived and said he had come to console our family. He approached me while I was sitting in my brother's room, asking me if I was okay and telling me that if there was anything I'd like to ask I should feel free.

I responded with one word: "Why?"

"Why what?" he asked.

"Why was he this way?"

"Because we are all born with original sin, and we must deal with the suffering that it brings," he answered. I had a big issue with that response.

"Sin my ass," I said as I stood up. "He didn't deserve this," I added and walked away.

I hadn't quite pulled myself together from the death of my friend and now here I was back in the pain that accompanies death. I didn't deal with my brother's death the way I did Jake's. This time death did not need to flicker into reality - it was as if I was drowning in despair until I could no longer breathe it in and I just stopped. This time I didn't say a word. Over the next few days, family, friends and neighbors came up to me, all saying the same thing, "We are sorry for your loss." An aunt, a neighbor, a family friend or one of my parents would ask me a mundane question or state a simple command like, "It's time to eat," and I would respond the same way every time, looking at the ground and walking away.

The funeral was on a clear day, hotter than I would have cared for, but at least it wasn't raining. I put on the same jacket I had worn to Jake's funeral only eighteen months earlier, got into a limo with my mom, dad and sister, and rolled down the road. For a brief moment I tried to make sense of what was going on. I was alone with my parents and sister, something that had not happened since I was eleven. We were dressed in the finest clothes we owned and riding in a limo much like we were on our way to a wedding. However, one critically different factor was the weight of the sadness that bound us together. Perhaps it was my family's strength in a time of great emotional strife that made us the same. We didn't lean on each other; we didn't try to cheer each other up. We'd all had years to prepare for this moment and I imagine we responded to it as we had each rehearsed separately in our minds. Most of it played out for me as I had imagined except for small details like not wanting to talk or the fact he died a few days before Christmas.

During the funeral I sat in my pew and rode out my emotions by focusing on the statues of Jesus hanging on the cross and wondering what his family must have felt. Time began to slow and my mind went silent. At the end of the ceremony my dad came up and said, "I want you to be the last one to see him." That's when I knew it was over.

I certainly didn't expect that request, but it quickly got my full attention. I walked to the top of the altar, knelt down in front of Anthony and looked at his face for the last time. All I could think was how amazing he was, and how I wished I could look into his eyes one more time. Then I stood up and walked away. A small ceremony was held by his graveside, but I couldn't hear much of what was said due to the ringing in my ears. I was also distracted by my body, which felt as if it was vibrating. As I walked to the limo from his grave I became very dizzy and everything around me just stopped for a moment. Then time slowly began to move forward, and I lost sense of what was happening. A neighbor I had only seen once before, came running towards me with a grimace of pain. She lunged to hug me and I put my hand up, then watched as she slowly fell backwards onto the ground. Several people gathered around to help her up as I walked to the limo without looking back.

I only visited Anthony's grave once after that day, and it was a reminder to never to do it again. A body that trapped a beautiful mind buried in a place he had never been didn't represent my brother's memory; it was only a painful reminder of feeling helpless.

Finally, all of the aunts, uncles, cousins and friends went home, and we were left to fill the void. Night after night I hoped Anthony would come to me in a dream and speak, but he never did. Days turned into weeks and I started to say a few words. A month later my parents explained to me that it was time to deal with his death. So I did. I never spoke a word about him to anyone. His memory has slowly worked its way through my mind and now he's part of me. I only wish I could remember him solely with fond memories, but that would diminish his existence. Anthony represented hope and happiness in the face of pain and suffering. A thirty-two pound, seventeen-year-old boy who lived each day isolated from the very things that we considered normal, and did it with joy in his heart. His life showed me we're meant to be happy.

I can't imagine what my parents went through during those days and the strength to make the decision they did. Regardless, it affected them for many years. It affected all of us. My mom kept as busy as she could and my dad went back to work. I went back to my apartment along the train tracks and finished community college. I spent a lot of time thinking about Anthony and I knew how lucky I was to be his brother. His sacrifice made me who I am and I am eternally grateful. I can only hope in time I'll find another piece of him hidden inside of me.

Experiencing death alters our life by adding limitations, obligations and confusion. Until the moment we face our own limitations we believe our life is endless. In reality, our time is limited and developing a desire to have an impact on the world around us is critical to our growth and our perspective on reality. When our personal growth begins to slow, time seems to pass more slowly, but when we're engaged in the world around us time seems to accelerate. The speed at which time passes has a direct correlation with the growth of understanding. Time is our compass for growth.

IV

PERSPECTIVE

We can see the future in our past, but we can change our future today.

Perspective is our window to the world and it is only blurred by our reflection. It holds the keys to our freedom by filtering out all that is difficult, allowing through only what is possible. Or it can be the shackles of our mind limiting us from our potential by only allowing through what is difficult, leaving no room for possibilities. Good from bad and right from wrong are choices that we make based on our experiences and from that we make our decisions. When we lack the experiences to make a clear choice it results in making decisions based on our instincts and replacing experiences with common sense. *Perspective accelerates the growth of understanding.* The greater our perspective, the deeper our understanding, and it is through the eyes and experiences of others that we can gain that perspective.

The next few years I lived in a small apartment within walking distance of the University of Central Florida campus. I went to class in the morning and I'd sit in the shade under a tree by the reflection pond at the center of campus in the afternoons. I'd read, glancing up from time to time to observe people as they passed by. It was the perfect routine and helped me feel like I had a future again. My weekends were spent mostly with friends at a football game or listening to a free concert, but the most fun was in the heat of a Saturday afternoon playing rugby for the University.

The nighttime was quiet and inspiring. I'd step out into the humid night with a pair of headphones on and run. On my runs I was drawn to the distant lights of the campus. I'd run between the buildings and pass book-carrying students as they left the library. Down past the fraternity and sorority houses there were always people coming and going and calling out to each other. It was a time of order in my life and it was an opportunity for me to exercise my mind and my body, but most importantly it was a time for me to catch my breath. Everyone should feel that experience.

As I got closer to graduation I began to wonder what I would do when this time of my life was over. Joining the military seemed like a logical choice but that idea was put to rest over Christmas dinner with my family when my father unexpectedly announced that he was heading to the Persian Gulf and there was a good possibility that there would be a war. He assured us that he would be stationed at a base far from any of the fighting and not to worry. When dinner was over and the plates were cleared I said my goodbyes and my father followed me out the door to my car. We stood in the driveway for a minute and he looked up at the night sky and said, "Do you remember when I brought home that telescope and we looked at the moon together?"

"Yeah," I said.

He looked down at the ground and said, "I always wanted to be a great father and at that moment I felt like I was."

"You are a great father," I said

Then he looked me directly in the eyes and said, "I don't want you joining the military. Your mother couldn't handle the thought of losing two sons, and she doesn't deserve to worry about it."

"Okay. But why do you feel it's okay for you to go?" I asked.

"I've made a career out of keeping this country safe and this is part of it." He put his arms around me and with a hug he whispered, "I have no idea what's going to happen."

I hugged him as long as he would let me, I told him I loved him, and I got in my car and drove away with him still standing in the driveway. Part of me wanted to believe everything was going to be fine, but based on the experiences of my past I assumed there was a chance that would be the last time I'd see him alive, if at all. I had become accustomed to loss by this point in my life.

One month later I sat with my mother watching the war unfold on television in the comfort of our home. We would listen to reports of missiles directed at the base where my father was located and my mother would leave the room every time the air raid sirens would begin to sound. When the sirens stopped I'd call out and let her know, and each time she returned wiping the tears from her eyes. I began to understand why my father had made the request he did. My mother could not handle the stress of another loss so soon after my brother's death. Without my father's request I never would have considered my mom's perspective, and it made me think about how my actions directly affect others whether it was my intention to include them or not.

To my surprise and relief my dad returned alive and well within a few months and was greeted with a hero's welcome by his small family. We spent hours talking as a family about the good times and sharing our memories. We talked about our old house and neighborhood, spending time with my grandmother and picking apples to make pies for Sunday dinner, and just enjoying each other's company. The feeling of having him home in such a short period of time with a great victory for our country was a tremendous relief and made me believe that this was in fact the greatest country in the world. My father's return proved that not all difficult situations will end in tragedy, changing my perspective by creating hope for the future even in difficult times.

Four months later I received my college degree and found out the degree alone left me under-qualified for every decent paying job and over-qualified for all the rest. Desperate to find something to pay the bills, I left the degree off my application and got a job forty-five minutes from home peeling shrimp in a restaurant for six dollars an hour. Fortunately, I never had a problem with working hard - it makes me feel like I belong to something bigger than myself. The good of the community versus the good of the individual was an ideal that my parents ingrained in me through their actions. When discussing the world, our country or our family, my father would state, "We're as strong as our weakest link. When I work I don't believe in being that link. In fact, I've always been the first to say, 'I'll do it.'" So that's what I did. Over the next two years I did anything that was asked of me from cooking to scrubbing the dumpster. I worked no less than seventy hours a week and I was sweating for most of them. I made enough money to pay my bills and eventually saved enough to buy a Jeep.

My forty-five minute commute each way, six days a week would take me down Route 50, and it was on that road where I spent a great deal of time pondering my life and life in general. One stretch of that drive always cleared my mind and made me feel good. The trees aligned tight to the road and were thick enough to form walls on either side of the winding two-lane route. It felt like driving through a tunnel and towards the end I would take a deep breath and hold it, waiting for the moment when the trees gave way to the wide-open space of the Everglades before I'd exhale. As the sun rose, a pink and orange glow cast itself for miles over the marshy green wetlands, hugging the bottoms of the clouds, and the only sound I could hear was the humming of my tires on the pavement. If I timed it just right, there was a five-minute stretch of road where all I could see was the sunlight glistening off the water and I felt at peace. This experience added a new perspective to my reality where just being in the moment was fulfilling.

After two years of restaurant work I wanted a job a little more rewarding than just collecting a paycheck. One of the guys that I worked with told me that he got a great job in the medical field and he was giving his notice to move on. I told him if they ever needed anyone else to let me know. Two months later he called me and said a position was open if I was interested. I quit that day, and two weeks later I walked out past the restaurant's dumpster for the last time, heading for a new opportunity.

There was no interview for the new job. I just showed up for my first day of work, which consisted of a quick lesson from the owner of the company on the simple art of performing an overnight pulse oximetry test. Her office was a single room with bare walls, a large wooden desk directly in the center of the room and a closet door behind her.

"Hi. I'm here for the lab tech position," I said.

"It's yours," she said in a nasally voice and handed me a clipboard with forms to fill out. When I was done I handed it back to her and she took a pager from her desk drawer and handed it to me.

"Here's what you do," she said brusquely. "Wait for this to beep, then call the number on the screen. You'll get a name, an address and a phone number. Drive to the address and tell the person the doctor said they need to take a test."

"Okay. What if they say no?" I asked.

"The test is to qualify them for Medicare so they can keep their oxygen. Tell them no test, no oxygen. It's a pretty easy sell. If they don't believe you, show them the doctor's number on the pager." She handed me a square canvas bag with a shoulder strap. "This is a pulse oximeter," she said, waving her hand over the bag. "It tells the doctor how much oxygen is in the patient's blood when they're sleeping. After they let you in, have them take you to their bedroom where you'll set up this oximeter next to the bed." She pulled a wire out of the bag with a finger clip on one end.

"This is a finger clip," she said, dangling it in front of me. "This is your bread and butter. Clip it on your finger, then have them clip it on theirs. That way they know it doesn't hurt. Then point to this button on the oximeter and tell them to push it and receipt paper will start shooting out the results from this open slot here while they sleep. When they get up in the morning, they should take off the clip and go about their business and you'll be by in the morning to pick it up. You sign the top of the roll and drop it off at the doctor's office. Each time you do that I'll pay you thirty bucks. You still want the job?"

"Sounds easy enough," I said. She handed me three oximeters and I slung them over my shoulder then symbolically clipped the pager to my pants and headed towards the door. "Any advice?"

"Try not to get caught in a conversation. These people will talk your ear off."

The next two years of my life revolved around this job, but not just because it paid my bills. I was given the opportunity to see life through the eyes of complete strangers at the most difficult times of their lives. The people I met and the way they lived ranged dramatically, but they all had something in common. They were either struggling with their health or they were caring for a family member or friend who was struggling to stay alive. I tested hundreds of people that were in the final years, months and sometimes hours of their life. My time with each of them was brief, and I considered it an honor to be there during that time. Every one of them had a story to tell about life from their perspective and I was fortunate enough to be their audience. I didn't know yet how these experiences would shape my perspective, but they did, and it gave me the strength to take control of my life.

It began with my first call, which came within 24 hours of turning on the pager, and I was out the door with my name, address and pulse oximeter. I don't remember the name or the address but I certainly remember the man. I walked up and knocked on the door of the house and an older man opened it up. He sounded Italian and had a thick accent but I could understand him just fine.

"Hello," he said.

"Hello, I'm here because the doctor needs you take this test." I then held up the bag.

"You can shove that test up the doctor's ass! Who the hell do you think you are standing there like a damn moron holding that stupid bag?" Then he closed the door. I stood staring at the solid brown wood for a moment, not recalling this reaction being covered in training.

The door reopened and it was his wife. "Sorry, he's a little sick of taking tests," she said. "Come on in."

Her comment was certainly an understatement but I was glad to have her on my side. After the man calmed down a bit I explained to him, under his wife's supervision, how to take a pulse oximetry test. I was rather proud of myself for recalling all the steps under pressure. Just when I began to feel good about the job I was doing, the man put his hand on my shoulder and leaned in closely. I looked into the weariness of his eyes from only a few inches away. He was tired.

"This is not a living," he said pointing at the oximeter. He took a deep inhale and quietly said, "Do something with your life. Do something you can be proud of before its too late. Something with meaning. Don't end up like me."

"Okay," I said. It was a moment I didn't expect or understand at the time, but I heard him clearly in a way that resonated over the years.

The next call I got was considerably less heavy. It was a woman that wanted me to set up the test in her living room because that was where she slept due to the fact there was a giant snake in her bedroom. She told me it had been in there for months, she didn't know anyone that could get it out, and it was keeping her from her pictures. I asked if it was okay for me to look, thinking I'd put her imagination to rest so she could go into her bedroom. She agreed, so I walked into her room and began looking around. The walls were covered with pictures of people. Some photos were old black and whites but most were in color and all of them had different frames. These pictures were obviously important to her and my goal was to reunite her with them.

"It must have left because I don't see anything in here," I called out. As I turned to walk back out, I sensed something move next to the doorway and there it was. It was dark brown, about six feet long with a body as thick as my wrist. Its head was moving side to side, the rest of its body folded on top of itself.

I froze, stunned for a moment as my heart began to beat rapidly. Then I heard her voice from the other room. "Is it safe to come in?"

"Actually, not yet!"

"You see the snake?" she asked.

"Yes I do."

"Do you need a hammer?"

"I don't think so," I said, staring at it. Its head kept moving but its body was still. "Do you mind if I use the blanket that's on the bed?"

"Okay," she said.

I snapped the blanket in the air above the snake and let it land on top if it. It immediately stopped moving. Now that I had blanketed the snake, with my heart racing, I pushed it with my foot and when it started to move I grabbed it just behind the head. I held on as tight as I could then scooped up the rest of it in the blanket with my other arm. As I ran through the living room it began to twist around my arms and the woman opened the front door to let me out. Once outside I realized it would probably go back into the house so I dropped it into an empty plastic garbage can next to her garage and closed the lid. I went back into the house and I found her in the bedroom holding a picture clutched in her arms. She told me it was a picture of her husband and she had not seen it since the snake arrived.

"Well, it looks like we can set the test up in here after all," I said.

The woman, whose name was Betty, could barely pay attention to my explanation of how to run the test, but I did my best to make my point. The moment I stopped talking she stood up and began gesturing to different pictures, giving me brief descriptions of each. All of her memories were hanging on the wall and each one contained significant pieces of information in the story of her life. Betty's excitement was contagious and I began to smile watching her. I left still with a smile on my face, lifting the snake-filled garbage can into the back of the Jeep and letting it go miles from her house on the side of the road. In the morning I returned with her garbage can, and when she opened the door she was smiling. She threw her arms around me and pressed her forehead against my chest. She was happy.

Betty told her doctor what I had done, and after that my pager began to go off and the calls to roll in. I quickly built a reputation for being willing to go anywhere at any time. Every call was a glimpse into the life of a stranger and it opened my mind to the challenges of others. I was often greeted by raw emotion and challenging circumstances forcing me to take my work seriously. This job forced me to think beyond myself, broadening my perspective by including others' views into my reality, in turn bringing greater meaning to my life.

Running fast was necessary at times when dogs would appear from nowhere, barking and chomping their teeth at me as I walked up to a home. However, I quickly learned that staying calm was the most important aspect of the job. One elderly woman I tested lived in a rough neighborhood filled with rundown apartment buildings and tiny homes surrounded by chain link fences. I parked on the street in front of the apartment where she lived with her husband. They were very nice people but were surprised that I was there, which seemed odd until I walked outside to leave and found my car surrounded by a group of people. As I walked up everyone turned and looked directly at me. Someone asked what I was doing in their neighborhood and I responded by saying, "A very sick woman lives in this apartment and she needed a test, so I'm here."

A man twice my size with tattoos covering one side of his neck walked up to within inches of me and with a booming voice said, "What's her name?"

"Dora Jackson."

He nodded and said, "That's my auntie. Thank you."

He shook my hand then looked at someone behind me and said, "He's cool." The crowd immediately dispersed. It was an easy lesson; some neighborhoods need protecting, and if I was going into one I had to make my business known. After that, I bought a white lab coat and kept it folded in my glove box. If things looked rough when I pulled up, I put it on and never had an issue again.

There was another form of protection that posed a challenge as well. One day I went to the home of a woman who had been in a coma for weeks. A Native American man opened the door, his body filling the doorway. "What do you want?" he asked, staring down at me with one hand behind his back.

"I was asked by the doctor to run a test on the woman who lives here."

He raised his voice and said, "My mother is sick of taking tests. She's in a lot of pain."

"This won't hurt at all." I reached into my bag and pulled out the finger clip and put it on. "Painless. It's so insurance will pay for her oxygen."

"All right then. Please don't be alarmed as I disarm myself." He brought his arm around from behind his back and in his hand was an extremely large handgun. I walked into the house to see his unconscious mother propped up in the living room on a neatly made all white bed, wearing a white nightgown and surrounded with pictures of people and fresh cut flowers. It must have been difficult for him to see her in that condition knowing he was helpless to do anything other than to make her comfortable. Situations like this weren't easy because there was nothing I could do or say. I just performed the test on her motionless body and ignored the fact that he never actually disarmed himself and used the gun as a pointer the entire time I was there.

An element of surprise also came with the job. One time I walked up to a house that looked like it had been abandoned for years but when I knocked a little old woman answered the door and invited me in. The moment I entered a wall of heat mixed with a musty smell hit me in the face and my eyes began to sting as I walked straight into a corridor of newspapers stacked to the ceiling. I explained that I needed to set up the test in her bedroom and she very kindly led me back through a maze of newspapers telling me about the son she had lost during the war. We exited the newspaper maze into a narrow hallway with two open doorways. Inside one a pale skinned woman with long black and gray hair sat naked on a mattress in an empty room staring directly at us. The woman casually pointed at her and said, "That's my daughter."

The other door was to her bedroom. A twin bed in the center of the room was surrounded by dark wooden furniture stacked on top of each other and everything was covered in a thick layer of dust. She began talking about her son and the great war while I looked for a place to set down my bag. I kept looking back at the doorway to see if her daughter was following us when suddenly the woman began yelling, "Get out of my house! Get out!" When I turned to look she was holding a loaded revolver pointed directly at my face. My hands slowly went up as the weight of the gun slowly pulled her hands down. Unsure what to do I just stood there while she continued to yell and point the gun at me. The thought of running crossed my mind, but the thought of getting shot in the back stopped me. Finally, my training took over.

"Um. Would you mind putting the gun down? I need to show you how to take this test and you'll need to put on a finger clip," I said. She stared at me for a moment as if she wasn't actually aware of what she was doing, then put the gun down in the dust on the dresser. She sat on the bed, looked me directly in the eyes and held out one finger. Her mind returned to the present and I taught her how to take the test.

It's natural for us to reflect on a difficult situation and personalize it to gain greater meaning of the experience. It is also difficult to step back and remove ourselves from the equation and view the experience from someone else's perspective.

Sometimes I'd get an address that would send me an hour or two out of town. These were often the most enjoyable experiences since I loved to drive and I'd stick around a little longer to listen to stories about peoples' lives. I spent an entire afternoon once listening to a man who had black lung disease from working the coal mines his whole life. He told me about all the places he'd lived working for different mines and how miners are great people who treat each other like family. If he had it to do all over again, he said, he would – despite suffering with black lung from the constant exposure to coal dust. He said with a slight laugh, "I used to climb mountains when I lived in Colorado and now I struggle to take a few steps. Let me tell you, there's always a price to pay with anything good." That man had strength within him and a perspective on life that my mind could not comprehend.

One time I had to take a dirt road for an hour that ended in the middle of an open field with a single faded blue and white rusted trailer surrounded in knee-high grass with an old pickup truck alongside it. I walked up to a screened-in area with no roof and it was lined with shelves, every shelf filled with parts from something. The voice of a man called out for me to come in. I walked into the kitchen and had to navigate my way around a pile of garbage, the stench so powerful I had to pull my shirt up over my nose to keep from gagging. I pressed on towards the back of the trailer where I could hear him wheezing as he struggled to breathe. Sweat began to pour from my forehead and was dripping onto the floor as I passed into what was once a living room to find him shirtless lying in the dark on an old couch inches below an open window with a fan that moved so slowly I could see it collecting dust in the sun light.

"Pardon my mess," he said politely, holding out his hand for me to shake. He looked to be in his fifties, but his body told a different story. His stomach was swollen to a point that his skin was stretched and purple and a fog in his eyes led me to believe he was blind. He gestured towards an old television with a picture of a smiling round-faced woman sitting on top and told me it was his wife who had passed away a few months ago. When she found out she was dying she had cut the picture from her driver's license, had it blown up and framed for him. As I looked closer I saw across her cheek half the Florida state seal. I knelt down beside him in the shadow of the turning fan and listened as he told me the story of their love.

It began when they were so young that they never knew life without each other. They married as teenagers and lived in that trailer, working together at the grocery store, had good friends, and never once had an argument that lasted more than one hour. Their only sadness was when they lost their first child on the day she was born and they never tried again. When his wife was close to passing he promised her he would take care of himself but he was too heartbroken to even try. He told me that he now lived only in his memories where she still spoke to him. He knew what she would say to everything he thought so he would talk with her as often as he wanted.

"When you have love in your life like ours it never ends. We're still connected and death has only made it stronger. I'm sorry you came all this way for no reason."

I thanked him for sharing their story and asked if there was anything I could do to help him.

"Tell whoever sent you that I wasn't here."

So that's what I did.

One type of call always filled me with mixed emotions and it always started the same way: "I have three for you in a nursing home." I knew that two hours of my time would make ninety bucks, but there's a price to pay with anything good. The nursing home runs were tough because everyone there was in bad shape and most didn't know what was happening or were completely unconscious. The people who cared for them always seemed to be understaffed and overworked. They seemed to be moving nonstop from the time I walked in until the time I left, and I always had a great deal of respect for them. I'd tell the person at the desk who I was there to see and with a smile she would tell me the room numbers and point down the hall. Guideless, I would walk the corridors searching for the correct rooms. All the doors were open exposing every person in the room. I imagined it made it easier to do rounds when you didn't have to open every door. All I had to do was walk down the hall, make three stops, turn around and leave the way I came in. I only made that walk a few times a month, but the experience stuck with me much longer. It was impossible not to notice everyone. I would do my best to look forward but it was inevitable that I would take in my surroundings – like passing a car accident on the side of the road, only it lasted longer and I could see everyone's faces. Partly I looked because I knew that someday that could be me and I'd wonder what it must be like to be waiting, alone and in pain.

Most everyone would be lying on his or her back but a few people would be sitting up and they'd look back at me. Depending on their eyes I looked away or made some kind of acknowledgement. The odor was often hard to bear but nothing tore through me like the sounds. Each of my footsteps echoed in the hallway, and the clang of equipment was often present, as well as calls for help. It seemed about a fifty-percent chance that I'd hear someone calling in a monotone voice, "Help, help." or "Help me. Help me." I asked a nurse once why they didn't rush in to help and she explained that the people were calling out for help but not from the staff.

Although my job was often emotionally challenging, there was always a lesson to be learned. The first time I went to test a person who had AIDS I was told repeatedly by the doctor's office to be overly careful and wear surgical gloves. Despite all I had been through with this job, I was actually nervous on the drive over to his house. I'm not sure what I was expecting but when he opened the door he looked fine to me. He held out his hand and with a big smile said, "Welcome." When I held out my hand his smiled disappeared as he stared at my sweat-drenched rubber glove and pulled back slightly.

"I was told to wear these for your protection."

"I'm not worried," he said.

I pulled off the glove, dried my hand on my shirt, looked him square in the eye, and shook his hand. Everything changed at that moment and we were just two strangers joined in a situation that we both didn't expect. He was actually interested in how the test worked and was the first person to ever ask me about myself. We talked for about an hour until his partner came home and greeted me with a smile as well. I actually left their house with a better perspective on my life. It was an incredible moment for me and I was honored to be there; I can only hope it was for him as well.

The most memorable experience of all started out the most simply. I pulled up to Edith's modest home with a manicured yard and a stone walkway that led to a front doormat that read, "Welcome." Edith answered the door and invited me in. I introduced myself and immediately noticed her walls were covered with pictures of smiling people. She was cleaning the entire time I was there and seemed to be in good health for a woman who looked to be in her eighties. As I explained what I needed her to do she politely nodded but it was obvious that she wasn't overly interested in what I was saying. I finished my setup and told her I'd be back in the morning, but she requested I come back in the late afternoon because her family was coming that night for dinner and she would be up late.

It was clear in my mind that Edith had no intention of running the test and I'd have to come back again and I was right. When I returned the next afternoon the street in front of her house was lined with cars and two women were talking on the front lawn. As I approached the house one woman said to me, "Are you Frank?"

"Yes I am," I responded, a little surprised.

"My mom asked me last night to tell you she was sorry that she didn't run your test and to apologize if she seemed preoccupied while you were here. She said you were very polite."

"Thank you," I said. "Where is she now?"

Tears welled up in her eyes and she said, "She passed away last night. After dinner she sat down in her chair and said 'I need to rest my eyes,' and she was gone." Her lips began to quiver and she said, "Thank God we were all right there with her."

When I entered the house to collect my equipment people were sitting around talking and as I passed through the house they all made eye contact and gave me modest smiles. Out the back window I could see children collecting flowers in the yard and calling out to each other. I wondered if they were playing a game.

After two years of being invited into the lives of complete

strangers, one fact could not be overlooked. The people who had family and friends in their lives were the happiest. As for those with no one in their life, that appeared to be the hardest of all. I was lucky to be part of so many lives close to the end. Every moment was a gift to me that made me stronger and gave me a better understanding of how to live my own life.

After those two years, fifty thousand miles and hundreds of memories, my ride finally came to an end. I got a call on a Tuesday and the owner told me that we were doing such a great job she had sold the company and the new owners would be calling me soon. They never did. With little savings and bills to pay I got a job loading trucks at a tire warehouse because I wasn't qualified to do anything else. Perhaps, it was a chance to let my mind get caught up with the past two years. As I worked, I thought about all of those people and how each one made some lasting change to who I was. While sweating in the back of a semi the one statement that I was holding in the front of my mind was the very first one I'd heard: "Do something with your life. Something you can be proud of before it's too late."

One night after work I decided to take a long drive, something I hadn't done in six months. After an hour of driving under a star-filled sky I arrived at the beach, got out and sat on a rock and listened to the ocean. I was hoping I would have a moment of clarity that would lead me to the next phase of my life. While I sat there I began to feel a calmness wash over me and I noticed that there was now an object in front of me that appeared to have washed up on shore. Then I realized it was slowly creeping up onto the sand. It was a sea turtle and it worked its way up alongside me as I sat motionless and watched. It began to dig a hole and then it moved over the hole and went into a trance. I was looking directly into one of its eyes and that's when I realized it was laying eggs. I watched her for a few minutes until another turtle coming out of the water further up the shore distracted me. It was then I realized there were many more all around me all moving on instinct and somehow all acting together.

Many of the people I met flashed into my mind and I could see their faces and hear their words and I could feel them because they were now a part of me. They each had lived a life, experiencing it from a single perspective, and this was my life and I was doing the same. We are all the same. My mind began to flash between two realities, one where I got up tomorrow and continued as I had today and one where I got up and lived guided by my instincts. The flashing between these two thoughts drew them closer together and at the moment they became equally real I changed my perspective and I began to believe I could create my own reality and live my life the way I thought it should be.

The next morning I got out of bed, put all of my belongings on the front lawn of my apartment and had a garage sale. I sold everything I owned for either five dollars or forty dollars and when I was done I had $385, some clothes, a can of disinfectant spray, two blankets and a wrinkled tie. I put it all in my Jeep and decided to take a drive to Colorado to find a mountain of my own to climb before it was too late.

If we continue to do the same thing as we've always done, our lives will slowly change allowing us to predict our future. If we choose to implement change in our life we can alter our future making it less predictable while shifting our direction. The more dramatic the change the greater the risk we take. How we perceive change is based on our understanding of the past and we call that perspective. Perspective allows us to have greater understanding of an experience and guides our choices. Having very little and no place to call home may be a difficult experience to some, while to others it is the highlight of their life. Perspective allows us freedom of choice.

V

UNDERSTANDING

There is only one truth and from that we grow.

When we look at the sun we see ourselves, and in the stars we see all living things. It is the energy of the sun that warms us and we are surrounded at a tremendous distance by so many like us. The distance should not stop us from knowing we're all the same; the distance is what keeps us all from becoming one. Understanding we're all the same but also unique allows us to exist independently making us at the very least part of something bigger than ourselves.

Understanding is the energy that constitutes life. We create this energy by sensing the information around us and interpreting it through our personal filters to create growth. This process begins out life and continues until we achieve something that cannot be explained by our current self – allowing us to alter our reality for the entire duration of our existence. Understanding is the product of life's equation. As I headed for Colorado, I didn't realize I was entering a period in my life where I would gain enough understanding to wake up and finally realize I was the only one in control of my life.

I drove thirty-two hours straight through the night, only stopping for gas and never thinking about what I had left behind, only about what lay ahead. The sun rose slowly behind me, casting the shadow of my jeep in front of me, leading the way to a new life. The new day quickly revealed itself with pink clouds on a light blue sky and a bright orange glow bursting from the base of the snowcapped mountains below. This place was my new home, decided one day on a whim – the place where I would create a new reality without judgment and filled with hope.

I arrived in Denver, Colorado in the fall of '94. Moments after reaching the city limits I went into survival mode, picking up the local newspaper and skimming the job postings for a restaurant opening and a room for rent. After two nights of sleeping in my car and driving from restaurants to random rooms, I secured a roof over my head for two weeks and a job cleaning squid for minimum wage at a hotel restaurant. Two weeks after that I got my first paycheck and an unfurnished one-room courtyard apartment on the outskirts of a Denver neighborhood called Washington Park. A mile away from my apartment, the large and beautiful urban park was filled with old trees, manicured grass fields, lakes, and an amazing view of the mountains. Every free moment I had I would walk the streets of my neighborhood on the way to the park, and often my eyes would well up with tears because I was so grateful to have started my own dream.

After a few weeks of squid cleaning, eating peanut butter sandwiches, and sleeping on the floor between two blankets in an empty apartment, my situation began to improve. One night I went to the dumpster behind my apartment to toss out some trash and saw that someone had discarded a twin box spring decorated in Stars Wars characters. I retrieved my can of disinfectant and sprayed it for a few minutes, then dragged it back to my place and covered it with the blanket from the floor. That discarded trash became my first piece of furniture and a way to get my body off the ground, making it easier to sleep. It became my anchor and it made me feel lucky to be home.

A few days later on one of my walks my situation improved again. I saw several kids playing in their front yard with pots, pans and dishes, thinking how interesting that these kids had such niceties to use as toys while I had none. Keeping my distance I asked if their parents were okay with them playing with their dishes outside. One boy responded, "Can't you see these are old junk and this is a restaurant?"

I reached into my pocket pulled out five dollars. "You know," I said, thinking fast, "some people sell their restaurants and buy ice cream with the money." He took the money and I stacked the dishes, pots and pans as fast as I could and headed in the other direction. When I made it back to my apartment, I put them in the dishwasher without soap and headed to the grocery to buy something other than peanut butter.

After a few months of my minimalist lifestyle I decided my dad was right - freedom is not based on what you have but the ability to be who you want. I could not keep doing what I was doing and hope my life would change for the better. I had to continue to change it. I looked in the paper for a new job and saw a position open for a night auditor working the graveyard shift at the Westin Hotel downtown. I had no idea what a night auditor did, but it had to be better than cleaning squid and hopefully would pay a little more. I put on the only button-down shirt I owned and finished it off with a wrinkled tie. All I took with me were the address, a pocketful of coins for parking, and a little hope. This move, this moment in time, was to become a decision that would change the course of my life once again. It was brief, it was unclear, but it was change.

When I arrived at the hotel I filled out an application and was escorted to the office of Brian Grubbs to be interviewed. Brian held out his hand and with a big smile offered me a seat. Looking over my application, he said, "Says here you're a squid cleaner. Why would you be interested in night audit?"

"I don't know what night audit is, but it has to be better than cleaning squid," I said. Just making the decision to change had already begun to change me. "I assume night audit involves adding and subtracting, which I know how to do. All I need is for someone to show me what to add and subtract and I'm certain I will do a very good job. Also, I'd be extremely appreciative of anyone who gave me a chance and I'll work hard to do it well."

"Well, makes sense to me. Let me explain the benefits," he said.

Just like that I was making one hundred dollars more a week and didn't have to shower off fishy odor every time I arrived home from work. The job offered several other perks that became quickly apparent. Once Brian had explained to me what to add and subtract I realized that I could do the entire job in less than three hours, yet I was scheduled for eight hours so I could run morning reports on a computer at 6:30 a.m. I used the extra time to read books that I checked out from the library on science and spirituality. My favorites were books involving Albert Einstein or Mother Teresa. I would sit with my back against the computer and read for hours until it shook back and forth as the reports began printing. When I got home I would lie on my box spring and read some more until I felt tired, then close my eyes. A few hours later I would get up and walk to the park. I followed this simple routine for nearly a year, and even though I was making enough money to buy a bed the thought never crossed my mind.

Now that I had made the decision to change my life for the better, I suddenly saw a chain reaction begin. Another opportunity appeared out of thin air, and because I was in the right place at the right time, my life improved again. Brian had explained to me when I started that we dealt with a lot of money, the hotel's money. If someone tried to take the money it was our job to figure it out and report them. He told me that if he wanted to he could take money but it was up to us to be honest. I thought that was an interesting way to explain the job so it stuck with me. Six months to the day of starting my night audit job, I was getting ready to head home with my books when the F.B.I. walked through the door and put the entire accounting department under house arrest. I was questioned by the F.B.I. along with everyone else in the department and told that Brian and his boss were asked to leave the building, which didn't necessarily mean they had done anything wrong. They asked if I knew of anyone who spoke of stealing money or if I thought someone was stealing. I remembered Brian telling me he could steal money if he wanted, but I also remembered how thankful I was that he had given me a chance and thought it wasn't my place to speculate or play hero. I said, "I work graveyards. I don't really know anybody."

It turned out that Brian's boss, unbeknownst to him, had embezzled over four million dollars. Again I felt good about my decision to be focused on what I understood to be true and not what I speculated could be true. Had I not done so on that day I would have felt guilty and foolish. I also would have suffered the loss of a lifelong friendship with a man who had believed in me. Brian returned to work the following week and I was promoted to payroll, making more money and working the day shift. My time had come. Now that I had a job making good money and a few new friends at the hotel I was asked if I'd be interested in sharing rent on a house in Wash Park that had been built in the early 1900s and was only a block from the park.

It was a chilly fall morning when I went to look at the house. Surrounded by large maple trees with reddish brown leaves, the house's front porch welcomed with a wooden swing. Passing through the front door and seeing the hardwood floors and custom tiled fireplace I knew I was home. I walked through the newly renovated kitchen and down the winding narrow stairs to the basement and saw a washer and dryer and an accordion door. I slid the door open and took my first look at what I would instantly know was meant to be my room. It had carpeting and a walk-in closet but most importantly it felt good. I went in and sat down on the floor and looked around. I began to think about all of the different places I had lived and got a strong feeling that this room was a place for me to start a new phase of my life. I started that phase with a question that came to me as I sat on that floor: "What am I?" With that simple question I suddenly understood that my desire to understand myself far exceeded any answer my current knowledge could offer. It was that simple. No fire in the sky, just a voice in my head assuring me that there had to be more. At that very moment I stood up, knowing a journey had just begun.

Over the next few months my perception of reality slowly began to break apart. My old world began to fade before my eyes and I did nothing to stop it. I threw away what I believed in exchange for hope. Hope that there could be more than just the world I see before me but a world right here and now that I had not yet seen.

I knew this journey didn't come with a built-in roadmap and I had only one idea how to accomplish my quest. I would start with a core, but first I needed to identify what I considered a core. I determined it would never be anything more than just me - "What I am." If I were to spend time focusing on the world around me or a world where I might want to go when I died, then I would get lost. I even prepared myself for the possibility that my existence was nothing more than a dream.

I also felt it was important to take other living things into account. In my short twenty-something years on the planet I was able to determine that we get what we give and realized it is our obligation to ensure a peaceful existence for all living things. Not just the things that exist now but for the right of all living things to come. What better premise on which to base my new reality? I had nothing to lose and everything to gain.

I had met many people in my life, most great and some not so great. I do find it interesting when certain people show up in my life. They revive me and bring a sense of self-worth that I cannot achieve on my own. Without the interaction of others my growth as a person would dramatically diminish – and it's all about growth. Without growth there would be no life, I believe. The physical world contains two things, life and everything else. If I can understand what I am, then I can understand a little bit about this world that can't be found on a slide under a microscope.

My new journey included many more books on religion, philosophy, poetry and science. I analyzed my past and my future and opened my mind to all voices, allowing myself to choose what worked best for me. What felt right would be the umbrella to my new reality. Science made me feel safest since it was rooted in facts and is often logical and can be explained. Physics specifically opened my mind to new possibilities since it deals with energy and motion. I also like ideas that can be expressed logically so they can be clearly communicated and easily reproduced. From that standpoint, I chose to apply analytical structure to my creative mind. I even decided to begin working on computer systems – something I knew nothing about – because I knew they were rooted in logic and would improve my analytical skills. So many roads beckoned when I started, but they all led me to the same conclusion – there is only one road to the truth, and that road was within us.

I began to walk a tightrope of self-absorption and social consciences. I wanted what was best for those around me and at the same time what was best for me. I continued to read, started running again, kept a good diet and even tried meditation. After reading up on meditation, I began to practice every morning before work and every night after reading. I was focused on taking care of myself and opening my mind.

After many months of being disciplined with my routine I decided to take my new life choices a little further and began a fast. I had no idea what I was doing but it seemed simple enough: Don't eat for five days and drink a lot of water. The first day I lay in bed with a pounding headache as my system began to adjust. The second day was easier on my body but mentally was a bit more straining. But the third, fourth and fifth days were easy. I began to feel great not just physically but mentally as well. I had accomplished something I wasn't sure I could do and I felt great about it.

I once read that praying was the act of asking and meditation was the act of listening. Meditation did not come easy to me. I became distracted very quickly but I was determined to achieve what is called an empty mind – a mind with no voice in my head pulling me in whatever direction it wished. I felt if I could achieve an empty mind then it would prove to me that I was more than just my mind, so I could gain greater understanding of what I am.

Two days after fasting I was still walking on a cloud physically and mentally. That night I went to my room and put on some meditation music and lay on my bed. While I lay there I began to have overwhelming feelings of gratitude. I found a peace in myself that I had never felt before.

As I lay very still, images began to jump into my mind and thoughts began to conjure up in my brain, but I watched without effort or judgment. I gave them no energy and they began to create themselves. Images of my life, my past, people I knew and people I'd never seen before. I watched as if I was taking in a movie. The images raced by as if to try to grab my attention but I refused. In fact, I offered no conscious effort to do anything. I just lay on my stomach, detaching myself from the entire experience as the images in my mind began to switch faster and faster until suddenly it all just stopped. As quickly as it had started, my mind went from the strobe-like effect of the images to complete silence. For the first time in my life no inner voice spoke in my head. My mind was blank. I was completely alone without a single thought to judge or give energy to. It felt as if I was floating.

Then, slowly, a single vivid image began to form in my mind of my family around the dinner table when I was just a child. We were moving in a sort of slow motion with my brother smiling directly at me from across the table. As I viewed the image I began to think about us living in our house and sharing experiences but each of us from a unique perspective. None of us were able to encompasses all perspectives; in fact the thought of doing so was beyond the realm of my comprehension. While analyzing this image I had a sudden realization that what is true to me is determined by my interpretation of an experience independent of what others believe to have transpired. A sense of tremendous responsibility filled my mind with the understanding that my truth is unique to me, and therefore I must understand my views and take ownership of my reality.

All of these thoughts were crystal clear and my eyes were fixed across the room. As I stared blankly at the wall, I began to feel a shiver in my feet that slowly worked its way up my legs. I was extremely aware of the sensation and the only thought I had was, "Whatever this is, I'm ready." That thought would be the one that set me free and sent me down a very distinct road.

The shivering feeling crossed my waistline and moved up into my back and chest. It felt as if my body was falling asleep without me and perhaps that's exactly what was happening. I maintained my focus on the wall in front of me, struggling to not move or even blink. I kept looking forward at the room I was in as the shiver made its way up my back and washed up over my head. My entire body was vibrating at that moment and all I could hear was a loud ringing in my ears, and then I experienced a flash-bang.

I could feel my lungs struggling to take deep rapid breaths. Suddenly a blue dot of light appeared. As I watched, the dot slowly began to grow before my eyes. It grew enough for me to realize that it was not a dot at all but a ball of light. It was a three-dimensional sphere glowing cobalt blue.

As I continued to gaze upon it, I noticed the sphere was no longer growing but was moving closer to me. My lungs began to heave as I began to gasp for air. The ball hung before my eyes what appeared to be two feet away and about the size of my fist. Then it began to fan outward, altering its shape and in the center taking on the form of a woman's face looking directly into my eyes. As I returned her intense look I felt the vibrations surge in every part of my body, my heart pounding in my chest and my face beginning to feel tight. At that moment I believe I was terrified. I felt no oneness with the universe or sense of being all-knowing. I was experiencing only fear and confusion. I was petrified. Even as I registered my intense fear, she finally closed her eyes and the ball folded in on itself and began to move away, suddenly disappearing.

My body began to calm, and soon I felt nothing but stillness within me again. Then my first thought was of my brother and how much I still loved him long after his death. In fact I loved him more now than I had when he was alive. That thought was quickly followed by the thought of my friend Jake, and I realized that I loved him as well. But in high school when we were friends I don't think I had ever experienced feelings for him that could be considered love. We were friends, and at that time I didn't understand that friendship was a type of love.

I began to realize that I was having a moment of clarity, experiencing a higher understanding of life. That was what this experience was all about, I suddenly knew as I realized, in such a profound moment, that relationships continue beyond death and that love for my brother and friend continued to grow. In that moment of profound thought I was humbled when I heard a woman's voice say, "What you are feeling is their love for you." I was stunned. I had actually heard a voice not within my own mind but from outside of me, perfectly clear.

The vibrations returned and I began to cry as I felt the hopeless pain of death - the desire to have one more moment with those who have died. All I wanted was one more moment to tell them how I feel and that I love them. The voice spoke again. "You have one more moment with those who are still alive," she said. "Now close your eyes and breathe." I closed my eyes, took a few breaths, and fell asleep.

When I awoke the next morning, I felt as though I had aged five years. I was not the same person I had been before flopping on my bed the night before and I couldn't tell if I was dreaming or awake. It was as if I had been blind my entire life and now I had seen a pinhole of light. I got myself ready for work the same way I would have on any given Tuesday, but this time I was aware I was doing it.

We only know one reality – the one we've determined to be true. Seeking to better understand ourselves, each other, and the world around us allows us to grow as living beings in search of our truth. When we alter our reality to include change we open ourselves to new possibilities and a more dynamic future. The ability to change is within all of us but the choice to do so depends on what we believe to be true. We are all the same.

VI

CHOICE

Reality is an illusion that trickles in the streams of our mind.

Reality is the seam that binds our imagination to all living things. Once the seam begins to unravel anything is possible if we maintain our focus. In the strength of our beliefs we see what is real and when we all agree we share in that reality. Our individual understanding of reality allows the freedom of choice in the safety of others. I had reached a fork in the road with two distinct paths. One path would be to live within the normally accepted version of reality and the other to explore an unknown reality from within. After some thought I chose to explore – although not right away.

I had spent years trying to understand my life at a more detailed level and now that I finally had an experience that opened my mind, I chose to take a break. I would fall asleep with the television on every night because I did not want to have that type of experience again anytime soon, but I still could not get that night out of my mind. During the day I began to imagine seeing blue balls of light. I would be in the middle of a conversation at work and I'd see a blue light floating over the person in front me or around their hands. I would become distracted and stop talking, but when I tried to look directly at it, there was nothing there.

In an attempt to distract myself from thinking about the strange experience I'd had, I started going out with friends and took on an extra job at work taking care of the computer systems. I began to work late into the night and if there wasn't enough to do I would read until I could no longer focus and then pass out from exhaustion. This routine continued for months until I finally found the greatest distraction of all, Rebecca. She was as beautiful as she was smart and we began to spend most of our free time together. Within a few months we became great friends and I even began to think that maybe she was someone that I could spend the rest of my life with – but at the very least when she appeared, the balls of light disappeared.

The moment my lease was up I moved out of the old shared house in Wash Park and into a downtown apartment by myself that had an incredible view of the city. Rebecca and I would head into the mountains on the weekends to ski or ride bikes. During the week we went to work and then spent most nights together at my apartment. The routine made me feel normal again and I put my journey inward on hold. As much time as I spent with Rebecca over the next eight months I never felt there was a right time to tell her about the night my world had changed forever.

On one of our trips to the mountains we got a flat on my jeep and during the process of changing the tire an officer pulled up and was kind enough to ask me if I needed any help. "No thank you," I said, but what happened next started a chain of events that had been in the making for over a decade and sent me in a direction I could never have imagined possible. He asked me for my driver's license which I happily handed him. He took it with him back to his car while I finished changing the tire. Just as I stood up, he walked back over to me and said, "We have a problem." Turns out I was the only one with the problem.

My driver's license had been suspended for years and I had no idea. The last time I'd had a ticket of any kind was eight years prior and it was for a taillight out. I didn't know what was going on, but I stopped driving immediately and since I lived close to work I started walking every day. The following week, Rebecca drove me to the DMV to clear up this obvious misunderstanding and get my license reinstated but again, things weren't going my way. After waiting in line for hours, when we walked up to the desk I was told that my license had been suspended in New York eleven years ago. Colorado had found out about it and suspended my Colorado license a year after it was issued, unbeknownst to me. When I called the New York DMV I was told I had to wait six weeks for them to pull the records to find out why it had been suspended in the first place because it was so long ago.

Two weeks into being unable to drive, I went for a ride with Rebecca to pick up some fabric from a shop in a small strip mall in the suburbs. I was grateful to have someone take me somewhere that wasn't within walking distance of my apartment. As we approached the mall, I noticed a reptile pet store two doors down and with an "I'll be in there," directed to Rebecca, I veered off and opened the door to the jingling of bells. I was immediately mesmerized the first time I saw a chameleon up close. I loved the way they rocked back and forth on the branches of their enclosures. I was watching one that was moving downward on a branch and its colors began to get darker, a purple stripe appearing on its face and then running down to its tail. I was watching how its eye moved around in a circular motion when I noticed it was looking at me. It was interesting how I felt connected to this creature so much that I felt hypnotized.

When I asked at the counter if I could buy him, it turned out that little guy was sold but there was a pair of Pink Panther Chameleons arriving from Florida in four weeks. They were two of twenty captive born in the United States and when he showed me a picture of them I instantly said, "Sold! I'll take them both." Like a little kid anticipating his first pet, I immediately bought everything I needed to build them a home. Setting up the tank in my bedroom was a great part of this experience. I built them a working fountain so they could see their water and I surrounded it with all different colored leaves to give them places to hide – and, I hoped, to make their colors change. I hung a live plant from the ceiling above and left the lid off the tank. I felt they needed something living to climb onto as well as the feeling of freedom. I finished it off with two heat lamps to keep them warm and a fogger to give them the humidity of their native climate. After it was complete I would lie in my bed and listen to the fountain as a thin layer of fog floated across the bottom of the tank curling in on itself at the corners. I stared at the tank for hours, counting the times I would see the light from the lamp above glisten in the fog below. This vision made me happy and I felt at peace.

Exactly six weeks to the day I called the New York DMV again and the agent on the phone promptly informed me that three years after my accident I had been sued by the insurance company of the other driver. Oddly, that insurance company turned out to be the same insurance company I had at the time of the accident. Although they had written me a check for the damages to my car and remained my insurance company for the next ten years, but for some reason had no record of me being insured by them.

Ironically, the insurance company that I had been paying religiously for the past decade to cover me, had sued me as an uninsured motorist, claiming I was responsible for all damages. The voice at the other end of the phone finally said, "You'll have to pay the twenty-thousand-dollar settlement before you can get your license back."

"What if I don't have twenty thousand dollars?"

"They'll set you up on a low-interest payment plan," she said.

"How do you know that?" I asked.

"It happens all the time. There's a guy in Oklahoma with the same situation as you who just started paying on a forty thousand dollar settlement. He has four kids and drives an hour each way to work. His wife drove him for a few weeks until the kid's school started. But without his license he would have lost his job, so he started paying."

"How do you know this?"

"I gave them my number and told them to call if there was anything I could do. They called me every couple of days and told me what was going on. I'll give you my number too."

"Are you my contact person?"

"No and don't let anyone know I gave you my number. I'm just trying to help," she said.

That night I went to bed confused and fighting off anger. In the middle of the night I opened my eyes and got out of bed. My room was dim, and I knew immediately what was happening so I opened my eyes and got out of bed but it was still dim. Again I opened my eyes and got up, until after the third or fourth time I would wake up in my dream only to realize I was dreaming. A switch inside of me had turned on so I was aware of what was happening but remained in this loop unable to wake. Finally I was able to free myself and woke up gasping for air. The last thing I wanted was to fall back asleep. I looked out the window until the sun came up wondering why that had just happened.

A few weeks later Rebecca drove me over to the airport to pick up the Pink Panther Chameleons while I rode in the passenger seat. When we arrived at the pick-up office a few other people were there waiting for deliveries. A mother and her young daughter were reading a book together in the corner; a man in a jumpsuit leaned against the wall near the office door. As Rebecca and I walked up to the counter, the clerk told us the flight was delayed and we were welcome to wait. The mother in the corner looked up and said, "We've been here an hour already. Our dog is on the same flight."

"I guess I shouldn't feel bad since I just got here and I'm only waiting on a couple of lizards."

"Lizards! What kind?" her daughter asked, jumping off her chair and walking towards us in her blue rain boots decorated with a pattern of white puppies. To pass the time I decided to tell the story of going to the pet store and seeing the chameleon looking at me. I explained what the two new chameleons would look like and how I'd built the fountain and left the lid off so they could feel free. The man in the jumpsuit was surprised to hear there was such a thing as a pink lizard and said he was going to have to see that. The girl asked her mother if they could see them too and she agreed. We waited together for another thirty minutes until the man at the counter called out my name and said my package was ready. I signed something and handed me a box and I placed it on the floor where everyone could see. I opened it and saw a blue bag labeled "heat warmer," but it was ice cold. I took the cold bag out and placed it on the floor. Inside was a smaller box. I lifted it out, opened it and moved a piece of padding aside. At the bottom of the box two ghost white baby chameleons lay motionless on their sides.

"Mommy, are they dead?" the girl asked.

"Looks like it," she said and they backed away slowly. Rebecca walked up to the clerk at the counter while the man in the jumpsuit continued to lean against the door by the office. The mother sat down with her daughter and I reached into the box with my finger and lifted one of the lifeless bodies out and placed it in my palm. I stared at its cold motionless body for a moment then realized that I felt a connection. Cupping my hands together, I began to breathe on it. After thirty seconds I looked up at the girl in the rain boots and held out my hand. Holding onto my thumb was a baby chameleon with its head up and changing colors from white to faded pink, continuing to a brighter pink with shades of purple. The girl held out her hand and the chameleon crawled onto her tiny finger while her mom supervised. I reached back into the box and lifted out the other hypothermic traveler. I cupped it in my hands and breathed a few times then held my cupped hands up to the girl and said, "Breathe on it." She leaned over with the other chameleon still holding her finger and with one breath I opened my hands and there stood a small white baby chameleon looking directly into the face of a smiling young girl. An hour later I placed the two baby lizards in the world I had created for them and they instantly turned it into a home.

Later that week I finally got through to the right person at my old insurance company. She explained she couldn't help because they were the ones who had sued me but she could put me in contact with a company that would set me up on a low-interest payment plan. "No thanks," I told her. I hung up and called a lawyer instead.

That night it happened again, with me waking up over and over in

116

my dream. After that it started happening once a week then quickly increased to several nights a week. In fact, it began to happen so frequently that I started to learn how to deal with it. It was always the same. If I got out of bed and the lights were dim I would jump onto the floor or knock things over hoping to startle myself awake. After several attempts I found a way out of the difficult situation by drawing Rebecca into something she wasn't prepared for. I discovered that when stuck in a loop if I yelled as loud as I could I would start making a moaning noise that would draw me out of the loop quickly. Unfortunately for Rebecca the moaning was loud enough to immediately wake her up and she would begin to shake me asking me if I was okay and telling me to breathe. I would still gasp for air when I woke up, but now that I possessed the ability to free myself from this nightmare, I was able to calm down quickly and fall back to sleep. That new ability marked my first step towards accepting what was happening.

I'm not entirely sure why I reached a breaking point but I was no longer able to hold off my mind and I began to tell Rebecca what was happening, including the voice and the blue lights. She accepted all of what I told her without question – in fact, she never asked anything. I told her about my idea of understanding being living energy and when I saw a blue light I'd point at it, but she never looked.

After that she didn't stay over as much though she listened to my stories and dealt with my moaning without a complaint or a comment. Feeling like we were starting to drift apart, I asked her if she ever thought about moving in together and that's when she decided to tell me what she really felt about all of it.

"I care for you and have thought about living with you but I'm not sure where this is going," she said.

"Are you asking if I want to get married someday?" I asked.

"No," she said, "I think you have some things you need to work out."

"Like what?"

"Like the nightmares."

"I can't help that."

"Can you help talking about hearing voices? Or pointing at invisible blue lights? You can't drive and you spend most of your time sitting at home staring at lizards. That's not normal. You need to get a grip and I'm not sure I'm ready to go there with you."

"I will say when you put it that way I can see your point, but you've got to trust me, I'm fine," I said.

We sat down on the couch, I held her hand and talked about the reasons why we should be together. It was a tough situation because I didn't want to lose her but my mind was shifting away from her and only focusing on what was happening to me. I decided to try to find a balance between her and my mind. I told her I would only pursue my thoughts when she wasn't around. It was a selfish attempt to create a false happiness, which went directly against everything I knew to be true. I was choosing to deny my true self to the very person I said I cared about, which wasn't fair to either of us.

We decided Rebecca would have a key to my place and she could come and go as she pleased. The arrangement worked well for about a month. The conversations about blue lights stopped and if I moaned in my sleep, she'd wake me then pretend she was still sleeping. Once I knew she was sleeping I would write down my ideas and then tuck the notebook between the books on the nightstand. I began to create drawings of what I thought living energy would look like and eventually started working on a simple formula that would represent the diagrams mathematically.

Had I known the impact the blue light would have on my life, I might have closed my eyes and turned away, but there was no turning back. I got out of bed each morning and wondered if today would be the day everything made more sense, but it never was. I became distracted from the world and spent most of my time thinking about something that I believed to be real or at least thought was real.

Rebecca went away for a weekend and since I still couldn't drive I decided to go for a walk downtown. It was overcast and cold and the streets were empty of people. I walked for an hour looking up at the buildings, watching cars surge from traffic light to traffic light. I even got lucky and saw steam twisting into the air from the holes of a manhole cover. I was a few blocks away from my apartment when the skies opened up and in a moment I was soaked and could see my breath clouding the air in front of me.

My eyes began to fill with raindrops and when I wiped them away I saw a street corner preacher delivering his sermon to the air in front of him, so I walked over and joined his congregation. I stood and watched as the man twisted his body back and forth, speaking of an almighty God and the heaven that awaited us if we accepted Jesus as our savior. Suddenly, I began to see myself in this man. He had a passion for something that he believed in and he had desire to make it real. The act of standing and listening gave him what he was looking for and he turned his dripping face in my direction and looked me directly in the eye. "I'm talking about your soul," he said, his deep voice booming. I stared back into his eyes and felt a vibration begin to wash over me as an idea came into my mind that finally made sense: my soul. The man returned to his sermon preaching into the cold damp air; that was all he had to say to me.

I rushed home to consolidate my ideas into a single document with the hope that if I read it and it still made sense then maybe it was true. I borrowed a ten-key calculator from work and picked up a few spiral notebooks, colored markers and pencils. I sat on the floor of my room, pulled out my notes, and started drawing diagrams of what I thought living energy might look like as I began working on an equation. I grew more excited as I worked, because the more pictures I drew the more it made sense.

I began taping the different drawings around the room until the walls were covered with pictures of dots connected by lines and with colored numbers written on each page. I also spread them around on the floor to make more room as I hammered on the ten-key for hours looking for a consistent equation. I wrote late into the night, stopping to sleep only when the sun came up. When I awoke I looked across the room and it was covered in drawings, spools of receipt tape from the ten-key littering the floor, and Rebecca was standing in the doorway.

All she said was, "This is not fine. This is not what normal people do!"

But it wasn't her words that made me realize she was right, it was her look. Disappointed, hurt, and worst of all, confused, I followed her to the door as she took the key to my apartment off her key chain and handed it to me then opened the door and left without saying good-bye. I stood there silently, knowing anything I said would hurt her more, and at the same time realizing that actually I was tired of hiding my truth from her. I was humbled by my decision to let her go because I chosen something in my mind over something that existed in front of me.

After six months, two thousand dollars in lawyer's fees, and twenty-one phone calls to the woman at the New York DMV, I was able to help my old insurance company find the error in their record keeping. On a beautiful fall morning, as the leaves were beginning to change, I got my license back. At the same time I knew I was committed to my path. Perspective became my window to the world and I held myself fully accountable for my perspective on the world. Falling in and out of love, being treated unfairly, listening to the words of a street corner preacher and witnessing a miracle in the eyes of child were all connected in my mind. They were the push I needed to commit to a path for my life. I chose to live by my beliefs even when the choice is a difficult one. I also chose not to let my circumstances define who I was but the challenges I had to overcome. Most importantly I chose to let others join me in the experiences enriching my life and hopefully the lives of others around me. Like a child holding a chameleon for the first time after just bringing it back to life.

I got in my Jeep and drove towards the mountains. As I drove, a vibration began in my legs, slowly working its way up my body and a feeling of freedom welled up inside of me and I began to cry. Every choice I made from that day forward was filled with the hope I will always live my life by my truth and clarity. The truth I had spent years searching for was written down in a paper that *did* hold together the next morning and has been instrumental in directing my basic life philosophy from that day forward. I titled the paper *Understanding Is the Energy Which Constitutes Life* and it is Life's Equation.

There is a unique reality that exists for each living thing but our life's energy is the same for all. It's our understanding.

VII

Growth

We are many that believe we are one.

Growth is a purpose not a state of being. Being is the many combinations of pieces we display in the moment. Every piece of understanding we've learned throughout our lifetime is at our disposal. We display them in different combinations based on our circumstances. Those pieces belong to us and not even time will take them away. It's when we set our pieces down that we open ourselves to growth. Finding growth throughout one's lifetime is difficult because we choose to stand in our own way. Energy growth is the driving force in our life. Growth is the highest form of acceptance and allows us to travel a great distance in a short period of time.

If we could project ourselves into the future we'd be faced with the harsh reality that the part of us that made it possible to stand in that future space was now just a piece of who we are. But we don't remain static – we must live every moment in search of growth knowing someday we'll outgrow ourselves. Sacrificing ourselves for growth is a debt we can't ignore. Having created my life's equation, I realized I couldn't afford to be complacent. It was time to start creating relationships with other people because I now fully understood my growth rested in their experience as well as my own.

I decided that it was time to be the best part of me and fully follow through on what I believed to be true, opening my mind completely without any expectations. The sensation reminded me of being six years old again hiding in the woods behind my house. Again, I was left alone in a world that required me to think to make it real. Except thinking in this new world was more exciting than when I was as a kid because it was my reality, and my life was filled with options.

I threw myself into my work on the hotel computer systems, which to me felt a lot like working on cars without the grease. I loved my new career because it was logical and I found that learning something new was as easy as just trying. Soon, the logic I applied to my work began to spill into the rest of my life. Each evening on my way home, I began to observe the drive differently. Instead of looking at the trees lining the road and wondering how and when they got there, I would notice they resembled an upside down lung as viewed from the inside - which made sense as it's the most efficient design to maximize gas transfer.

I began to question things I had never thought to question before –

such as "Why do I need to eat?" I also took notice of how interesting the experience of eating was and how I'd never really paid attention to it. I had paid even less attention to my own breathing, probably because I did it all the time so focusing on it would be a distraction. But if I did focus on my breathing, working to consciously slow it down, I discovered I could control my thought process much more effectively. The most surprising observation of all turned out to be the least obvious. Drinking water regularly made perspective on a situation more positive regardless of what was happening at the time. The lack of water had the direct opposite effect. These functions were all so simple – and ones I had been performing my entire life – but I had never before thought to take notice. I was finally present.

I walked away from any talk of material objects or perceived success, replacing them with talks about experience, different perspectives, and the dreams of others. Relationships and the understanding of all living things became the focus of my time. I only engaged in relationships where I had something to offer and I had the opportunity to gain the experience of another in return, then I measured my success on the speed of time passing. If time appeared to speed up, I knew I was gaining new understanding at a rate faster than I had been. All of my relationships became important because they represented an existing connection and the possibility for energy growth.

Working for the hotel provided me with many opportunities to build relationships, beginning with people staying the night, whom I just observed. Others stayed for several nights and some would visit often enough that I knew their names. I also developed relationships with people working at the hotel. Some worked there and left before I met them, while others I grew to know very well. Those I didn't know well provided me the best opportunity for developing a new relationship and further broadening my understanding. Little did I know one such relationship had so much potential that it had a profound effect on my life.

Roughly once a week I'd get a call over the radio from the office by the loading dock to work on a computer that was acting up. I would gladly leave my room full of servers and take the elevator three floors down to the basement. The elevator opened into a cinder block hallway with beige painted walls and I would follow the faded path in the linoleum floor towards the loading dock. As I passed housekeeping, I would receive smiles and waves from everyone restocking their carts with the mini-sized bottles of shampoo and bath soap. I would smile as wide as I could, repeating, "Hi" and "Good to see you" over and over as I passed through. Ahead, the steam from the laundry room poured out though the doors and upward, clinging to the ceiling as I continued past. At the edge of the loading dock was a stand-alone cinder block office. The fluorescent light inside flickered through a single wire mesh-reinforced glass window where I could see the back of a bald man's head partially covering the computer screen in front of him.

Opening the door to the office was my favorite part of the trip. I'd turn the knob and as the door swung inward, the chair in front of the computer would slowly turn to reveal the gentleman who monitored the dock. A stubble of gray hair framed his face and a complex series of lines surrounded his blue eyes. He was always dressed in blue overalls and wearing a broad smile. Embroidered in red above his left breast pocket was his name - Bud. When he saw me standing there, his jaw would slightly unhinge his smile and he'd say, "Howdy!"

Bud always stood up to look me square in the eye and shake my hand, and I could see the top of his head was covered in freckles and spots as he moved around to my side to allow me to sit down. He'd watch over my shoulder as I performed "my magic," in his words, to get his computer working quickly again. We always had enjoyable brief conversations that started out with him complimenting me on my skills and then moving on to all the wonderful people who worked at the hotel. The only words he shared with me about others were positive. It made me feel good to know that if he said something about me to someone else it would be positive as well, and I liked that about him.

One night I was working late and I heard Bud's voice calling over the radio, "Is there anyone there?"

"Yes, Bud," responded the night shift manager.

"Where are you?"

"I'm at the front desk. Where are you?"

"I don't know," Bud said. "Can you come find me?"

I listened to the conversation as it played out over the radio.

"Tell me what you see."

"Lines of doors," Bud said.

"Are there numbers on the doors?" and so on.

Bud was found within minutes. Physically he was fine but he was disoriented. An ambulance was called and Bud left for the hospital less than five minutes after he was found. I made it to the front drive in time to see the back of the ambulance as it pulled away.

The next afternoon I was back at work eating a turkey sandwich in the lunchroom when I heard that the hospital had given Bud a CAT scan that showed an inoperable brain tumor the size of a grapefruit. He was being transferred to a hospice and the doctors were giving him 72 hours to live. He was not coming back to work and he would not be going home again.

After hearing the news about Bud I couldn't stop thinking about him and the fact that I'd never made the effort to have a more involved conversation with him or learn about his life. It all seemed so final and I felt as if I had made a mistake. I went home that night and lay in bed for hours thinking about Bud, unable to sleep. Eventually my eyes began to sting and I closed them, but my thoughts continued to go around and around.

After what seemed like hours of random thoughts about Bud, I opened my eyes and the room was dim. I sat up, my body feeling so weak I could barely stand. When I moved it felt as if I was underwater. Light began to surround my vision and I could feel my heart begin to pound. I closed my eyes tight and when I forced them open I was back in bed. I sat up and looked around at my dimly lit room and immediately knew I was stuck in a loop. Over and over I stood up and ran in slow motion across the room. I'd yell without a sound. Jump without leaving the ground. I'd slowly throw myself against a wall, but each time I opened my eyes, I was in bed and still in a loop.

Eventually I gave up trying to break free and lay still in a slight panic.

This strange disorder had been with me as long as I could remember, it was getting worse, and I could not escape. I began to wonder if perhaps it was being caused by a tumor, which of course made me think of Bud lying in his hospice bed. Then I remembered the words I heard the night I saw the blue light: "You have one more moment with those that are still alive. Now close your eyes and breathe." I closed my eyes, took a slow deep breath and with a flash-bang it was morning and I was free.

I got out of bed that morning determined to go visit Bud at the hospice immediately. It was an interesting decision since I hardly knew him but it seemed to be the right thing to do. My past experience with the medical company had taught me that a brief visit from anyone to anyone in a hospice is usually welcomed warmly. I called the hotel, found out where he was and told them I was taking the day off. I took the top off my jeep to let the light of a spring morning warm my body as I drove an hour up the highway to where he was staying.

Arriving at the hospice, I stopped at the front desk and asked the woman if Bud was okay with visitors. The woman at the desk told me yes and gave me his room number. When I found his room, the door was open, which I knew meant he was under watch. Although dressed in a hospital gown and lying in a bed, Bud still looked the same. I gently tapped on the door and he looked at me with surprise. Couldn't really blame him since the computer guy he hardly knew was standing in the doorway during

his final hours.

"Howdy!" He said with a big smile and I felt relieved.

"Howdy to you."

"Thank you for coming to see me. This is a great surprise."

"I just wanted to stop by and say hello. I hope I'm not bothering you."

"Nah. I was just looking out the window at this view." He had a

beautiful full view of the mountains framed by two white flowering

crabapple trees on either side of his window.

"Come stand next to the bed. I want to show you something." I

moved around to his bedside and watched as his arm began to slowly float

out to one side.

"I'm trying to shake your hand and look at this. I think I'm in a bit of

trouble. I was told there's a tumor the size of a grapefruit that has caused

me to lose control of my right arm and leg. It's supposed to get worse, but

I don't think so since my head is only slightly bigger than a grapefruit now.

Huh?" He let out a laugh. "I've been exercising and I think I'm getting

better."

He grabbed his right wrist with his left hand and began to show me the exercises he'd created. He moved his arm up and down and from side to side. "Just like this," he said. I was surprised and impressed that he hadn't given up. I stood next to his bed and we talked a little about some of the wonderful people at the hotel while he continued to exercise his arm. After a bit of time passed a nurse came in and told him it was time to take his pill so I made that my excuse to leave.

"I can come back in a few days to visit if you'd like." I said.

"I'd like that a lot," he said. He held out his right hand with the help of his left and I set my hand in his and held it.

"I'll see you soon."

"I'll be here," he said.

On my drive back home I thought a lot about my decision to visit him. I had done the right thing. It was right for him and it was right for me.

Three days later I got off from work and headed up the highway to see him again. When I arrived I asked the woman at the desk if Bud was still there.

"Yes he is," she said with a smile.

I took her cheerful response as a good sign and headed for his room. When I entered his room I noticed it was much the same as the first time –

just him in his bed alone staring out the window. The sun was setting between the flowering trees and the evening light spilled into his room turning his thin frame into a shadow surrounded by an orange glow. I walked up and whispered, "Hey Bud. How are you?"

He turned his head slowly on his pillow to look at me and raised his right arm from beneath the sheet, holding his hand out as he said, "Howdy."

"That's incredible. You did it!" I said and began to laugh in disbelief.

He then gestured with the same hand to a chair near the window and said, "Sit." He propped himself up on his elbows then slid up in bed, dragging his right leg and looking out the window, his face glowing in the now amber light.

"I've been thinking a lot about you." He said. "Why do you think you decided to come see me?"

"I'm not completely sure. It just seemed like the right thing to do."

"There's something more. Everything is for a reason. We just don't know what that is yet."

Bud began to tell me a little bit about himself as we watched the sun dip behind the mountains. He had grown up in Pittsburgh and moved to

Colorado for work after the war, hanging power cables and installing transformers. He met his wife when he was climbing down from a pole. She was just standing there. They never had kids. They always wanted them but just couldn't have them and never knew why. His wife, Beth, had passed away more than a decade ago. He no longer needed to work but had started working at the hotel to keep his mind active.

"You can learn how to live alone. Being alone, that's easy. Missing her..." He stopped himself from continuing, covering his mouth with his hand. He stared out the now blackened window and focused on a distant street lamp holding its own in the dark of night.

I took that as a sign it was time for me to go. Once again I told him I'd be back in a few days and he said, "I'll be here."

I headed down the highway, gazing up at the stars, and felt I'd see him again. He was well past the doctor's expiration date and he seemed to have his mind made up that he was sticking around for a while.

One week later I drove back without calling ahead and walked down the hallway without checking at the desk. This time when I walked into his room it was different. His bed was unmade and he wasn't in it. I was standing in the doorway wondering if our story had reached its end when I heard someone approaching.

"Howdy," he said from behind me. I turned around and there he stood.

What do you say to something like that? "Great to see you too and by the way, how is it possible that you're standing, not to mention alive?" Bud was getting better and that was reality. His sheer determination to get better had enabled his brain and body to find another way to work together. His motor skills had been restored and he was well past the doctor's seventy-two-hour prediction. I was witness to a miracle.

He extended his hand and I took it. "There's something I want to show you," he said. Without a word he led me down the hallway, shuffling his feet side by side and moving at an even pace. We arrived at the cafeteria where people were sitting at round tables with a variety of meals and drinks between them. They were conversing, animated and smiling.

"I've made a few new friends. It's important to do that, you know," he said. He began to use both hands to reference different people. One by one he went around the room and told me their names followed by their kids' names if they had any. Then he moved on to where they lived, what they did and why they were there. He was telling me about a woman who was thrilled she'd just gotten new skivvy britches the day before and asked him if he'd like to see them. I began laughing at that story but he just continued around the room in more and more detail on each person.

Eventually I found myself just staring at him in amazement as he continued to describe each and every person in great detail. He had a profound ability to consume information about others and recall it that made me realize he wasn't just the nice man from the cinder block office but an absolute genius.

When we returned to Bud's room, he sat on the edge of his bed and said, "It's your turn. Tell me about you and I've got time."

I told him how I'd found a job at the hotel after moving to Colorado from Florida. I told him about my work at the medical company after I finished college and that my dad had gone to war after my brother died. I told him my best friend in high school had died the week after I was in car accident – a few months after I had stood in the eye of a hurricane. It felt good to tell my story, and I appreciated him for taking the time to listen. There was something very powerful about the way he listened. He made me feel as if my life mattered.

"So, you were a pallbearer at your friend's funeral? Tell me about that."

It was interesting he asked about that because I had thought a lot about what it was like at the time but had never thought about it since.

"As I helped carry my friend into the chapel, I was thinking that his funeral could have just as easily been mine," I admitted. "It sounds selfish but at the time I was thinking of myself. Perhaps everyone there that day was thinking the same way but I only know what it was like for me. My life as a child ended that day as I held onto my friend's casket. I just realized I was there with my life still ahead of me and, just like that, he was gone. Honestly, I never thought about that day again. That's what it was like to be a pallbearer," I said.

"I know how hard that can be," Bud answered. "My first job during the war was to be a pallbearer but not like you'd think. My group landed on a beach shortly after everything was over. At first it was hard for us to understand what we were looking at, but then we began to realize what had happened. We were ordered to bring anyone we found far up onto the beach and line them up. We worked in teams. At first there was no need to look for anyone because they were everywhere. We started out by lifting them off the sand and carrying them, but as the hours passed we all got so tired we began to drag them up the beach. I couldn't help but think if we had arrived a little earlier it would have been us too. We didn't talk about it at the time but I suppose we were all thinking the same thing. We were lucky to be alive and they weren't. You can't make sense of it." He looked down for a moment and when he looked up he said, "We now have a deeper connection. Your story made me think of a moment in my life from a different perspective so I told it to you. It's a bond we share and nothing will ever break it."

I went home that night and thought about his story and how it related to my experience. It made me reflect on that entire time in my life but most importantly I remembered who I had been at that time. I held those thoughts until I became very tired and drifted off into a loop where I sat up quietly in my bed then opened my eyes to see that I was lying down so I could sit up again. I did that for hours until the sun came up and filled my room with the light of day.

I returned to see Bud a week later with no expectations that he wouldn't be there, and not only was I right, but he was sitting outside on a bench with a blanket on his lap facing the mountains, watching the sunset. I felt great joy rise up inside of me at the sight of him, and I knew at that moment our relationship had only just begun. I walked over and sat down next to him. "Oh good you're here," he said. "You can walk me back in after the sun goes down."

"I would love to."

"Did you think about our conversation?" he asked.

"I did that night for a few hours until...I fell asleep. I thought about what it must have been like for you. Then I began to think about what it had been like for me, and the experience had a new meaning that it hadn't before. It was more important to me, if that makes sense."

"Makes complete sense. You fell asleep, huh? Tell me what that was like."

"Why would you ask that?" I was a bit surprised by the request.

"That was the only time when you were talking that you seemed unsure, which didn't make sense," he said.

"Fair enough. I didn't fall asleep I got caught in a loop." I waited for his reaction but there wasn't one.

"Okay. Keep going," he said.

"Sometimes instead of falling asleep I get caught in a loop. I think I'm awake but I'm not and I'm aware I'm not. I begin to force myself to wake up over and over but I can't. It's like I'm trapped. It's been happening to me as long as I can remember. It's like I'm losing control of my mind."

"Or finding it. Huh?"

"What?"

"Perhaps you're finding your mind. You talk about being aware it's happening. Are you aware of anything else? How it feels? Can you see?"

"Yes." I said. "I'm actually very aware of everything."

"Next time just take it in. Try to remember it."

"Why would I do that? It's not real."

"How important is love and being kind to others? Are they real? Is God real?" he countered. "Would people spend a lot of time talking and thinking about something that wasn't real? You've thought a lot about what you just told me. I know it's real and so do you. Next time just take it in and remember it."

"Okay," I said.

"Promise?"

"Yes," I agreed.

Bud had a wisdom that only comes from years of experience and contemplation. I was lucky enough to cross his path at a time when he was prepared to share his words and insight.

"I've lived a good life and I put my trust in God," he continued. "In my life I have been challenged many times and always did what I believed God would want me to do. The right thing. The choice that made the world a better place even if it wasn't easy for me. In return I asked God to trust me. I would like to have God trust me with the whole thing prior to my death so that I will know the truth about life even if it's just for a moment before I die. That's real. Huh?"

That was what he had thought about his whole life and that was what he was waiting for. His belief was simple and beautiful. The night grew chilly and I walked him in. When I left I told him I'd return in a week. He smiled and said, "I'll be here."

A week later he told me the nurses allowed him to go home for a few hours.

"I checked on a few things. Everything looked in good order."

When I asked him why he thought he was doing so well, he responded, "I've been asking for God to help. What else could it be?"

Made sense to me.

I returned to visit Bud every week. It became something I did without question and he was always there. The spring quickly turned to summer and all of our time together was spent building a relationship. We had known each other for years but it wasn't until the end that it really mattered. The more I learned of him the more my own life made sense. Each week we knew exactly how it worked. He needed to share and I needed to learn.

One week I returned and did my usual walk up the hall to his door –

except this time it was different. He was lying in bed staring out the window. His head slowly turned toward me and with the same look I had first seen four months ago he said, "I fell."

"Did you get hurt?" I asked.

"My hip. It's over for me. Just like that."

This was not the way I'd imagined anything to be. I'd always known I would hear those words come from his mouth eventually, but I wasn't ready. I responded the only way I knew, with hope. "Can you start over?" I asked.

"I wouldn't know where to begin."

"Just focus on your breathing," I told him. He held out his hand for me to hold. I took it and without a word we both closed our eyes and breathed.

I felt a bit numb so I tried to think of what I could do to help besides hold his hand. I decided to call on the voice in my head that I'd heard a year before and try to bring the vibrations back to me. I'm not sure why it seemed like the correct thing for me to do, but I was at a loss and that was what I had. This was my friend and I didn't want him to go. The vibrations never came but I kept hoping. I followed the rhythm of his breathing until we were breathing as one and after 20 minutes he spoke.

His eyes still closed, he began to whisper, "Help me God, help me God, help me." He began to speak it louder and with more desire. "Help me, help me, help, help." A shiver washed over me as he repeated himself louder and louder "Help, heeelp, heeelp." I closed my eyes and listened to his cries for help and it was then that I understood.

When I opened my eyes he looked directly into them and he said, "I've got this. I know what to do. I need to be alone right now. Thank you." I leaned over and hugged him and said good-bye. I told him I'd return in a few days and he said, "I'll be here."

I headed home that night and watched the sunset while driving down the highway. I was in pain. The tires buzzed on the pavement and the sun slowly dipped below the mountains. I didn't get off the highway in Denver - I just kept going. I continued south and watched as the moon rose and cleared a place for itself in the night sky. I thought about Bud, then I thought about myself. I pulled off the highway for gas and I wiped my tears before continuing south. A few hours later my heart went numb as the sun came up. My mind finally settled down somewhere in New Mexico, so I turned around and headed home.

I returned three days later and the receptionist stopped me to tell me that Bud had been unconscious for several days. I thanked her for the information, actually relieved he was still alive. I knew it wasn't going to be the same and this was going to be my last memory of him. I walked into his room prepared to say my final good-bye.

Bud was lying in his bed, eyes closed, and breathing. That was it: just breathing. He actually looked relaxed but his mouth was dry and his cheeks were very pale. I'd seen this look before and I knew what it meant. It wasn't easy for me to accept that our talks had reached an end. My final memory of him would be him without his voice. I sat by his side as I always did and was watching him breath wondering if I was going to witness his last breath. It was then that a minister or pastor or priest of some type appeared in the room and said, "Is this a good time?"

"A good time for what?"

"His last rites."

"Go ahead and I'll come back another time," I said.

"Please stay," he responded. "You appear to have a special relationship and I'm sure he'd want you to be here."

I agreed.

The pastor placed his hand over Bud's left hand and began to say a prayer from memory that consisted of heaven's gates, Jesus, and an angel. As I listened I realized that Bud never discussed religion. In fact, he'd never mentioned it or heaven. He'd only spoken of God and life. If that were true, then why was this man here saying something about an angel. I reached out and touched the back of Bud's hand while the pastor carried on in the background and Bud's eyes slowly opened. He looked at me and with a slight smile said, "Howdy."

"Howdy to you." I could not hold back the tears as I leaned in to get as close as I could to him for one more moment.

His next words were, "Who's that talking?"

"Oh, wow," the pastor said, obviously surprised that Bud was with us. "I am here to pray with you. Is that okay?"

"Sure," Bud said still looking at me.

"Do you believe in angels?" he asked Bud.

"Sure. Why not."

The pastor spoke again of angels and made a reference to heaven while Bud and I held hands smiling, then he left as suddenly as he had appeared. Bud whispered, "I need some water."

I quickly grabbed a cup and filled it. I lifted the back of his head so

146

that he could reach the cup in my other hand and he took a few sips, then let out a sigh that I took as a sign he was done.

"I'm so glad you're here," he said.

"I'm so glad you're here, too," I said, and we both let out a small laugh.

He then tugged at my hand and said, "I know. I know now."

It took me a moment to understand what he meant but then I asked, "God trusted you?"

"Yes." He held on to my hand with what little strength he had and closed his eyes. Tears began to roll down his cheeks and dripped onto his pillow as he spoke. "He did. He finally did. Thank you for everything you've done for me." He took several breaths, opened his eyes and tilted his head towards me, asking, "Is there anything I can do for you?"

I will never forget that question or the tone in which it was said. This man knew his life was about to end but thought he could still help me. Somehow our relationship would continue. In that moment I could only think of one thing.

"Can you please watch over me?" I asked. "I'm kind of alone."

"I will." He paused. "Come closer." He reached out with his hand and

I leaned in towards him. I could feel his warm breath on my face as he whispered, "I know who you are now." He took a few breaths and stared into my eyes, "Do you know how much I love you?"

"Yes."

He pulled me closer and kissed my cheek then said, "But I want you to promise me that you won't come back. Okay?"

"Okay."

"It's my time. I know now you can't come back."

"Okay," I repeated, making a gasping noise to catch my breath.

"I love you. Now promise me?"

"Yes." It was hard for me to tell a man who I hardly knew that I loved him but I did and then I cried.

I left that day and only made it up the road to an overlook. I stopped my jeep, turned off the engine and sat on my roll bar to watch the sunset. After a minute another car pulled in to do the same and then another and another. A couple in one vehicle got out and sat on their hood. Others got out and leaned against their cars, just watching. We all watched together as the sky began to glow. Through the tears in my eyes I saw the colors of the sky blur into the mountains below.

Two weeks later, I broke my promise to Bud and returned. Knowing that he might still be there was hard for me, but mostly I just could not let go. I asked the woman at the desk if he was conscious and I was told that he had not been conscious in weeks and would not gain consciousness again.

"In fact, he could go at any minute and if you're prepared for that, then it would be good for him to have you there," she said.

I agreed, even though I knew Bud had asked me not to come back. I walked into his room and sat by his side as I always did. I kept my breathing very shallow to stay as quiet as possible, watching him breathe for a few minutes, staring at the unchanging expression on his face. His mouth was open slightly and his eyelids were pale. Then his eyes began to slowly open, his pupils were dilated, and I could feel a pull at my heart as if it was being squeezed as he slowly whispered one word, "Promise…"

All I could say was, "I'm sorry."

I ran from the room. I rushed past the front desk and paused long enough to say to the woman, "He's awake."

"That's not possible," she said and started down the hallway as I headed out the main entrance for the last time.

One week later Bud took his final breath. It was six months, nineteen days and four hours after he'd been diagnosed with the tumor and given seventy-two hours to live. At the time he died I was alone in my dimly lit bedroom moving around slowly, feeling as if I were underwater. I put down every piece that was me and surrendered to my mind. It was not through my strength alone but keeping my promise to Bud that set me free. He was now a stronger part of me and I could feel our love as it continued to grow.

Who we appear to be at any point in time is based on the parts of us we choose to display. The present moment in time creates an illusion that allows us to believe we are one person, but we are merely shadows of our past, and relationships are our growth. These relationships are our connection to everything and define how we are viewed outside of ourselves. We share our understanding with others the way Bud offered me his wisdom and strength at the end of his life. It's only because of his willingness to share his life that I know what's possible. I am wiser and stronger because of him.

VIII

Connection

We get what we give.

Caring is what keeps us alive. Being cared for and caring for others. It's a principle that works with all living things. If we care for the life around us, then we will be cared for in return. If we care for the passions we possess, they too will grow, and we are brought a positive result in return. This idea is what we commonly refer to as Karma.

I don't recall being born, but I imagine it as overwhelming. A burst of light in front of me and then the hands of a stranger lifting my body from the fluids of my mother out through an incision in her abdomen. My skin tightened as it was exposed to the atmosphere of the operating room and I began to feel the weight of my own body for the first time. Only my voice filled my ears as I forced the breath from my lungs for the very first time announcing my arrival. Then I was placed onto a table and examined by others to ensure I had arrived safely. That is how I imagine I was born.

Six months later, wrapped in a blanket and clutched to my

mother's chest, she rocked me until my father returned home. Often late at night he would hold me in his arms while the sounds of voices from the evening newscast filled my ears. From the hands of caring strangers into the loving arms of my family, I was alive and everything was new to me.

In those first days I built relationships for the first time and they were all based on a love that exclusively comes from being cared for. It is the deepest connection, developed because it is the beginning of life and the only hope for survival. Those who sacrifice to care for another display the most raw and truest definition of love. It was time for me to develop deeper relationships while taking a greater risk with being true to myself.

Sometimes I feel an intervention from outside of me and I surrender to something bigger than myself. It's a connection to something I've felt for as long I can remember. I've ignored it for certain periods of my life, and each of those times my life has felt somehow less full. A blue light floating in the air or a vision in the darkness of a place I've never been represents a piece of me connected to something that I don't really understand other than the fact that it's with me all the time – whether or not I choose to acknowledge it. It is a mystery to me, and when I choose to foster the relationship with this uncertain connection, my world grows in ways I struggle to understand. One fact is certain: I am connected to this "other" and that relationship allows me to grow. Caring about a relationship with something limitless makes logical sense since we constantly grow our understanding.

After Bud passed away it became clear to me that I had not developed any meaningful relationships since my early years. All of my relationships after my brother died had been brief and without much depth. I had spent many years processing my own internal chatter, not committing the energy to try and understand others. I felt as if I understood people to a certain level of relationship that had become the way I defined all of my relationships.

I'd had many relationships in my early life that were rich but all had limitations. Family, friends, pets – all of these relationships expired so many years ago that I haven't kept track of their duration or, with some, that they even existed. But each of them is still with me and I use them to help me grow. The more value I place on each relationship, the more I receive in return. If I calculated the value of my past relationships then I would see that same value in other things around me. So, too, is true of the opposite. It's a fairly easy choice and the results are pretty clear.

In my late twenties I began to open myself up to everything and everyone around me. It was a period of time that I referred to as "waking up." It felt as if I was going into relationships deeper than I had before, and the more I did it, the easier it got. People started telling me about their lives and what they believed in. All I had to do was ask.

At the age of twenty-nine I was navigating a vast array of relationships. People I met just for a few minutes would willingly and enthusiastically talk to me about many different aspects of their lives, and I noticed that many of these relationships went in only one direction. I would ask a question and the person would tell me what they were willing to share of their understanding with no reciprocal or desire for another perspective. The relationships all ended in a "thank you" and we would each go our own way. I remember vividly on several occasions certain individuals becoming emotional when responding to a question I'd asked. When that happened I quickly put up a barrier, saying, "thank you for sharing," and we would each be on our own way. When we're asked to share in return is when the relationship really begins and true understanding of each other surfaces. It happens at all different levels.

The harder we try to launch a relationship, the more difficult it becomes to get out of, and often it's not worth the effort. But some relationships can be mutually beneficial. The challenging part is figuring out when and what or, who.

I recall sitting in my office at the hotel waiting for a new hire to arrive for hotel computer orientation. The orientation basically consisted of five minutes of me telling them what not to do and what to do if they did anyway. I always greeted everyone at the door. I felt foolish the one time I sat at my desk and reached across it to greet someone I didn't know. I wasn't sure if that was just my sense or if I was feeling a transmission of energy from their judgment of my gesture, or lack thereof. Needless to say, I never did that again.

This one particular morning, I stood in the doorway and watched as a woman approached. All I could see was the top of her head. Her hands were inside a purse slung over her shoulder. She stopped directly in front of me without looking up, her hands moving the contents of the bag around a few more times as she said to herself lifting her head, "I can't find anything in this bag..." Somewhat surprised to see me, she said, "Oh, hi!"

The moment we looked into each other's eyes I could feel myself breathing. Her smile turned my heart into that of when I was a child and my cheeks filled with warmth. I don't recall ever staring directly into the eyes of someone I didn't know for that long, but I couldn't look away. I felt physically connected to her and I didn't even know her name.

"I'm Frank," I said after a moment and held out my hand.

She took my hand and said, "Hi Frank! I'm Ashley."

The touch of her hand sent a vibration through my body and every movement she made seemed to be in slow motion. When she spoke the words rolled from her lips and I could see them as a visual in my mind. This connection was most certainly one I had never experienced before. Very little information had been exchanged between us, but there was no denying that time was slowing in the presence of this woman and I was growing rapidly. She created an energy in me just by looking into my eyes and my only conclusion was – we must be the same.

Over the next few weeks I'd see her in passing and without a word I'd hold up my hand and she would high five me as I passed by. The high five slowed over time until we would just pass each other and touch hands and exchange nothing more than a smile. I spent all of my free time thinking about her. She was the last thought in my mind when I went to sleep and the first thought I had when I woke up.

One afternoon, I was leaving for the day with my keys in my hand as she walked around the corner. I quickly held out my hand. As she approached time began to slow and I looked directly into her crystal blue eyes as they came closer into view. My heart began to race as she reached out to touch my hand, but this time my keys got caught on the sleeve of her sweater.

"Oh no," she said with a giggle as I quickly worked to disconnect them.

"I'm so sorry. I can't believe it." I was overwhelmed with embarrassment and wanted to run away, but my key ring had snagged her sweater and it was stuck. I began slowly working the threads free one by one. The only words I could find at that moment were, "Don't worry I'll get you a new sweater."

"That's going to be tough," she said. "It took my grandmother a year to knit me this sweater. Do you know how to knit?"

"No, but I can learn real quick," I said with a smile and we both began to laugh. She took the keys from my hand and unhooked them from her sleeve.

"Do you really think you can learn to knit a sweater real quick?" she asked, smiling as she returned my keys.

"Probably not, but maybe we could go to lunch sometime and you could tell me about your grandmother."

"Okay. How about tomorrow?" she said.

"Perfect. I'll see you tomorrow. Sorry again about your sweater," I said and started to walk away.

"You do know I was joking about my grandmother knitting it? I bought it years ago when I lived in San Francisco."

"Then maybe tomorrow you can tell me about living in San Francisco."

"I would love to," she said with a smile.

Ashley and I went to lunch the next day and each ordered the same salad from the menu. She told me about growing up in California and living in San Francisco where she'd managed a hotel. I told her about growing up in New York and moving to Denver from Florida. We took turns asking questions about each other and I was fascinated by her every word. She continued to appear to me as if she was speaking in slow motion, and when I spoke I had to force the words from my mouth. In the blurred background people were rushing by, their voices melded into one creating a shroud of sound all around us. We looked each other in the eyes through the entire lunch, never once looking away, not even to eat. Three hours later we got up from our table and walked off into a new world where we were connected and salads went untouched. There began a conversation that would never end.

That night, lying in my bed contemplating sleep, I couldn't stop thinking about her and how she made me feel about myself. I felt an energy inside of me that made me feel more alive than I could ever remember. For the first time I felt as if I wasn't alone. Closing my eyes, my mind began to drift as a vibration began in my legs and worked its way up my body until it washed over my head. I no longer experienced the fear I had in the past, instead feeling only curiosity and a strength I'd never had before.

With my body vibrating and my eyes open I rolled out of bed and stood on the floor in my dimly lit room and knew immediately that I was in a loop. It was the first time I'd felt calm and open to the experience, and I held up my hand to examine it, watching it move as if it was underwater. I moved around the room with little effort, my body seeming to be nearly floating. Everything in my room was in its proper place, and in my bed I could see myself lying on my side facing away from me. It was then my attention was drawn to a blue glow surrounding my bedroom door, and when I looked at it I felt at peace. The light grew brighter, causing me to look away for a moment. When I turned my head to look back I was rolling over in bed and the loop was over.

There are many events in one's life that are considered significant in the construction of who we are and the choices we make. Many of those events are impactful and often out of our control. It is as if an explosion has dislodged us from our complacent emotional and mental state, forcing us to go beyond ourselves and transform to something new. Then there are events that are much more subtle in nature creating a chain reaction of other events. Together, those events also take us beyond ourselves to become something new where we are in control of our direction. These types of events are a choice in the exploration of free will.

Over the next month Ashley and I spent every free moment we had together. We'd spend hours in Wash Park under a tree or sitting on a bench by the lake talking about our lives and asking each other questions. We talked about our pasts, our families and our dreams of the future. It was like two friends who had not seen each other since childhood trying to catch up. After four weeks of constant talking while sitting on the bench looking over the lake, she turned to me and said, "I think I'm in love with you."

"I know. I'm in love with you too."

Her eyes filled with tears and with a crackle in her voice she said, "Thank you."

It was then I reached out to touch her face and leaned in to kiss her for the first time. A shimmer washed up my body and over my head. I pressed my forehead to hers and said, "I've been waiting for you for a very long time."

The next morning I pulled up in front of her house in my topless Jeep and she came walking down the front path with a bag of clothes over her shoulder. She tossed her bag in the backseat next to mine and climbed in.

With a kiss to say hello we headed to the mountains to spend every minute of the next three days together. We held hands the entire way, giving a squeeze from time to time as if to say, "I love you," without speaking. Each time I looked at her I was in complete disbelief that she was with me; at the same time I felt as if she *was* me.

The sun was bright and the air warm when we arrived in Vail. We spent the next two days hiking, biking, and doing all the things two young people who've just fallen in love do. We didn't question that we'd been put on this earth to be together. On the third day we took a gondola ride to the top of the mountain with a blanket, two glasses from our room and a bottle of wine to watch the sunset. We found a secluded area that looked west out over the valley, the landscape filled with tree-covered white-capped mountains set beneath a cloudless blue sky. We laid out our blanket on a small patch of grass and sat the bottle and glasses on the nearby rocks, beginning a conversation that would solidify what we already knew – we were the same.

"Is there anything we haven't talked about it? It's been only a month and I feel like I know you better then I know myself," she said.

"I feel the same way, but if you really want to know, there are a few details I haven't mentioned," I said.

She looked at me with an excitement and said, "Don't hold back. Don't hold back anything. I want to know everything about you."

"Okay." I took a breath to calm my nerves before saying, "I'll completely understand if you ask me to stop or think it's weird."

"Now, I have to know," she said, turning to look me directly in the eyes.

Our time together had been so amazing and I truly believed we were the same. But I was also scared to tell her about what goes on in my mind and what I could see. But it was part of me, and if we were truly the same then she would understand. The moment I began to speak I couldn't stop.

"When I was kid I would be woken up in the middle of the night by a flash of light and a loud bang that would terrify me so much my entire body would shake for hours. I forced myself to stay awake all night for fear it would happened again," I began in a rush. "I spent a lot of time alone when I was young and sometimes I saw visions of places with people, who would see me and smile. And I would smile back at them." As I spoke I could feel myself getting choked up and stopped to take a breath.

"Go on," she said, her simple words giving me the strength to continue. I turned my head and looked out over the mountains and just let go.

I told her about talking to Jake in my dreams and how my mind would get trapped in loops. The vibrations I felt in my body, and walking around my room at night while my body lies in bed. I ended my confession with the blue lights and the voice speaking to me about death and love. Slowly, I turned to look at her face, expecting it to be filled with concern, but instead, her eyes were filled with tears and her mouth with a smile.

"I can see a blue light floating just above you right now," I admitted. "I don't know why. It's just what I see."

"Oh my god, you're a healer!" She looked surprised at herself as she quickly covered her mouth and said, "That just came out. I don't know why I said that."

"I like that better than 'you're crazy'," I said with relief. She put her arms around me and held on. I put my arm around her and we watched the sun as is it dipped behind the mountains revealing a star-speckled evening sky.

The next day I held her in my arms while we leaned against the railing of our balcony looking at the shadows cast by the mountains in the morning glow. We stood in silence and communicated by gently tightening our embrace and changing the positions of our arms in an effort to get even closer. After a period of time our breathing became synchronized. We had finally found each other and we weren't going to let each other go.

"We should come back here a year from today and get married," I whispered in her ear without a concern in the world what her response would be. She slowly rolled her body in my arms and stopped when we were sharing the same breath, then she stared deep into my eyes.

"Yes. Let's do that."

We pressed our bodies and lips together until we could no longer tell where my body ended and hers began. Our connection was finally complete – or so we thought. We packed our bags and left later that day with the promise of returning in a year to be married. But sometimes things change and some promises can't be kept.

Over the next month Ashley and I spent every moment we had together, inseparable, absorbing every word, every action, and every breath we shared. Our conversation never stopped and time began to slow so drastically when I was with her that I could feel the individual muscles in my face contracting when I smiled. When we slept we took turns holding each other all night until the day forced us to get out of bed. Item by item I began to move in with her. My apartment, my furniture, and the food in my cabinets had all become obsolete. I discarded what I had once placed any value on as mere objects. The only thing of true value to me was

Ashley – until the day she called me at work and said we needed to talk.

Working through lunch on the days Ashley was off allowed me to finish early and get home to her. That day, the phone rang while I was working on my computer holding a plum between my teeth. Seeing it was her, I stopped to answer it.

"Hey there."

"I'm sorry to bother you but I really need to talk with you," she said and her voice was a little shaky.

"Is everything okay?"

"I'm not sure. It can wait till you leave, but I needed to hear your voice now."

"I'm on my way." I hung up the phone, grabbed my plum and made it home in record time to find her sitting on the couch. Her eyes were red and she looked as if she had been crying. She normally greeted me with a smile, but not this time. She just sat on the couch rocking back and forth slightly. I sat down next to her.

"What's wrong?"

"I don't think it's right," she said.

"What's not right?"

"It's says it takes ten minutes and it changed right away so I don't think it's right," she repeated, holding out a positive pregnancy test in front us. The left side of my face began to turn very hot.

"I must have done something wrong. It can't be right," she said, handing me an egg timer that was on the couch next to her.

I thought it was odd that only one side of my face was hot. I'd never had that happen before, but then for some reason I started to wonder if she owned an egg timer or had just bought it.

"Are you going to say something? Do you think I used it wrong?"

"Did you pee on it?"

"Yes," she said.

"Then I think we're going to have a baby." It was then that both sides of my face returned to normal temperature and all I could think about was her.

"It's going to be great. Everything is going to be great," I reassured her as we sat on the couch holding each other, a pregnancy test, and an egg timer as silence passed. Finally, I held out the egg timer, examined it, and said, "Did you just buy this?" She let out a laugh and we were complete.

Our actions send a wave outward into the world around us like a ripple on a pond. Those ripples will eventually return to us in a force directly proportionate to the wave we send, and we must prepare ourselves for their return. How large a wave we choose to send should be equivalent to the willingness we have to receive that turbulence. Over time the waters will calm and a new clarity will be found. Knowing this to be true each wave should be sent with a selfless force of hope and humility.

Six months later Ashley and I got married in a small ceremony far from the top of Vail Mountain. We spent our free time converting a spare room into a nursery while reading books on birth and parenting. All talk of "us" quickly ended and became about the pregnancy and preparing for the baby. I found a new job with a software company that didn't pay much more than I was making but offered a lot more opportunity over time. Ashley quit her job and took a job working part-time from home so we wouldn't have to put our baby in childcare. Financially it was going to be difficult, but we decided it was a sacrifice we were willing to make.

Two months later, ten months after we met, our daughter, Camryn, was born. She was instantly swaddled and placed on Ashley's chest and from that moment on we were a family. That night, while Ashley was sleeping, I was holding Camryn in my arms alone for the first time. When I looked at her face I finally knew why I was put on this earth, and I began to care for her in a way that only a parent can understand.

From the moment we brought her home I looked for ways to connect as quickly as I could. I changed her clothes and her diaper as much as possible, sometimes when she didn't even need it. Between Ashley and me, we were checking or changing her clothes and diaper every fifteen minutes. When she was hungry she would cry until Ashley would feed her. At first it was difficult to understand where I fit into that equation until I began bringing her to Ashley every time she needed to be fed. No matter what time of day or night, I quickly became the 'blur' in Camryn's eyes that brought her to the other 'blur' that could feed her. It was only then I felt in complete possession of a relationship with my daughter.

Within a few months we found our routine as a family. I would leave for work in the morning and Ashley would take care of Camryn during the day. I'd learn as much as I could at my job and get home to them as quickly as possible. When I arrived home Ashley would start making dinner and give me the minute-by-minute replay of everything that had happened during the day while I held Camryn at the kitchen table. We'd eat. We'd feed her and put her down for the night. Ashley would go to bed and I'd stay up, sitting down at a computer in our bedroom and continuing from where I'd left off from my day at work. I'd write code until Camryn would wake up. Then I'd change her diaper and bring her to

Ashley to eat, then code some more.

By the time Camryn was six months old I was averaging four hours of sleep a night. Often I would go to bed because my eyes were too tired to focus but not because I was ready to sleep. I would just lie there with my eyes closed for an hour as my mind slowly wound down. In the quiet of the night, in the peaceful feeling of being home with my family, vibrations would wash over my body. Once the vibrations were strong enough and I could no longer feel my body I would begin to float. It was at that point that I could roll over and stand up next to the bed.

I would spend what felt like hours observing the dimly lit room around me. I'd jump on the bed to try to wake up Ashley then I'd jump off the bed so that I could slowly float to the floor. I would pick up everything I could find and examine it. Everything felt lighter yet somehow the same. I would reach up and touch the ceiling just by raising my arm. It was obvious to me that the limitations of my body did not exist and this experience was something my mind was creating. This type of exploration went on for months until it finally ended when the blue light returned.

After a night of working late I lay down in bed and was immediately engulfed in vibrations. I rolled over and sat on the edge of the bed. Our bedroom door was open slightly and a blue light began to fill the opening. It began to grow brighter and eventually a small blue orb appeared in the doorway and floated into the room. As it floated up to me, I followed it with my eyes the entire way. I felt a sense of inner peace that was undeniable and I just watched as it moved around me filling the room with a blue glow. When it began to head back towards the doorway, without a thought I began to follow it.

I left our room, following the light down the hallway and up the stairs to the main floor with me right behind. I moved into the kitchen and the room was filled with moonlight pouring in through the windows. For the first time I could see everything brightly and clearly. The light moved towards the backdoor and passed straight though it out into the backyard. I began to follow it and felt my forehead hit against the solid door I could not pass through. I paused for a moment and an excitement began to rise inside of me, my heart racing as I reached down for the doorknob. I turned it and pulled the door open and the light from the moon poured in around me.

I stepped out into our backyard and it was bright as daytime under a full moon that lit up the night. I could see the trees, flowers and grass. It looked exactly like our backyard in every detail. I walked down our flagstone path lined with flowers I had planted the weekend before. I unlatched the back gate of our wooden fence and ventured out into the neighborhood, walking for some time down the street just looking at my neighbor's houses, which appeared to look exactly the same. Off in the distance I began to hear sounds of music and voices, so I headed in that direction.

The sounds grew louder as I walked up the road, finally reaching the corner where multicolored tents lined the street with people milling everywhere. A three-piece band played in one of the tents and families walked with their children, everyone seeming to be having a good time. Inside the tents, smiling people displayed colorful jewelry and paintings of landscapes, people and cities. Continuing to walk down the center of the street, I was surrounded by people. A woman passed close by carrying a child on her hip. She looked directly at me and smiled. I smiled back.

All around me people of different ethnicities wore colorful outfits. Some were eating, and others were talking and laughing. A group of young children ran through the crowded street past me, each holding a glowing lantern made of different colored paper. At the center of the street I looked at the festival around me, and the joy that everyone expressed on their faces and in their actions began to create the same feelings within me. I just stood there until I heard a voice from behind me say, "Great to see you've made it."

I turned to see a man with short dark hair and a few days' worth of growth for a beard looking at me, and he placed his hand on my shoulder.

171

Dressed all in white, his shirt and pants draped over him in a delicate fashion, he smiled as if we'd known each other our whole lives.

"What do you think?" he said.

"It's wonderful," I said.

"Come with me. I have something you need to see."

I followed him without question as we slowly moved through the crowd, walking side by side as people let us pass by without noticing we were there.

"Who are you?" I asked.

"Your guide."

"Is this real?"

"Are you real?"

"Yes."

"Then so is this," he said.

"Where are you from?"

"Perhaps the next time we can go there," he said. We stopped in front of a tent filled with jewelry, and at the center of the tent was a young man sitting on a small wooden stool. "This is what I want you to see."

I stepped into the tent with him and the man on the stool smiled and held his hand out in front of me. In his palm was a bracelet made out of grass. I instantly felt a connection and remembered sitting in a box as a child making bracelets just like it.

"Take it," said the man on the stool. "I've been holding onto it for you. It's yours."

I could see my hand as it reached out to touch it – in disbelief that it really was mine – and I felt a sense of overwhelming joy that made my lips begin to quiver. The moment I touched the bracelet, my sight began to blur with tears. Then a vibration filled my entire body and with a flash-bang I opened my eyes and I was in bed.

That experience opened my mind to question everything I ever knew about what I believed to be real. Sitting alone in a box making a grass bracelet is nothing more than a stored memory of something I had done when I was a child. Leaving my body and walking through a festival was now a stored memory as well. Both memories were created from experiences I had with no one else there to validate them. Neither experience was created in my imagination nor would I consider either a dream. The question wasn't which experience was real, but what is true reality.

During this experience the basic laws of physics seemed to apply when I was not questioning them. The light passed through the door, but I had to open the door to follow it. If I picked up an object I felt it had a weight and I could touch it. But if I tested the basics of gravity by jumping I had a sensation of temporarily floating. When I tested limits of my physical body by reaching to touch the ceiling I was no longer bound by the usual rules. The fact that each experience ended with a flash-bang lends me to believe that I may have been capable of having these experiences my entire life – or that I had been having these experiences but had never before been able to store them as a memory. This experience appears to be one of two possibilities. Either I actually left my body and experienced another reality that exists where the laws of physics only apply when they are not questioned, or my mind is capable of creating a reality very much like the reality I experience every day and share with everyone around me. Both possibilities are extremely compelling.

I spent the next two years of my life staying awake as long as possible. When I got home from work Ashley and I would spend time with Camryn until it was time for her to go to sleep. Then we would spend time talking about our life together and how lucky we were to have each other until she went to bed. After that I would do everything I could to stay awake as late as possible. I taught myself different programming languages, studied for technology certifications and began creating software applications just for fun. It was an extremely productive time in my life but I did it mostly to achieve a state where I could vibrate out of my body several nights a week to explore a new and unlimited world.

It didn't take long for me realize I could go further by projecting my thoughts rather than walking, and once I did, my experiences became more exciting. I'd project to cities and over fields, focusing in to get a closer look if something caught my attention. Sometimes I would stop when I saw people and ask them questions to gain a better understanding of where I was and who they were. Some people offered a lot of information. They would tell me about where they were from and how they got there. Most of the people I talked with had a much better understanding of what was going on than I did, as if they had been there for a long time, while others ignored me or became irritated the moment I approached them. Some just stood there with blank stares on their faces as if they were extremely confused. I learned how to use my time wisely by exploring as much as possible and only talking with people who looked at me with a smile. I began living two lives. The one I always knew to be real and another that was becoming more real every night.

I began to talk with Ashley about my experiences but it certainly wasn't the most important conversation for us to have. We had a daughter to care for and a relationship built on love. The company I worked for was growing and they were paying me more than enough to cover our bills. We made a lot of new friends to spend time with on the weekends. It was a life that I couldn't have imagined possible and all I wanted was for everything to stay that way forever. But it did not.

I returned with a flash-bang early one morning to Ashley yelling my name from upstairs. I jumped out of bed and she met me in the doorway of our bedroom with a strange look of surprise. "Turn on the TV…"

We sat in front of the television and watched helplessly as the second plane struck the World Trade Center. Then we watched in horror along with everyone else as the first tower crumbled before our eyes followed by the other. Our perfect world was crumbling before our eyes while our two-year-old daughter handed us colored blocks off the floor. This disaster was a chain reaction of events of the worst kind and its impact on the world was unimaginable. Within days we heard the stories of the families that had been destroyed. A week later Bob, our mailman, was wearing a surgical mask and rubber gloves to protect himself from a possible anthrax attack. A month later we were at war in a country I knew little about. Six months later the company I worked for stopped growing as the economy began to slow. A year later lay-offs began, but I was told not to worry because I would be one of the last to go. I sat at my desk for months, watching people I worked with, good people with families just like ours, lose their jobs and their security.

Now at night after Ashley went to bed, instead of staying up as late as I could, I'd pick up Camryn while she was still sleeping and hold her in my arms. I would turn on the news and listen to stories of people losing their jobs, homes and their lives in war. I had no reason to complain, but any happiness I'd once felt about our future was replaced with uncertainty. It became a time in my life where I felt I was holding my breath waiting for the world to change and everything to get better. I held Camryn close and my fears even closer.

After a year of lay-offs my company had downsized by more than fifty percent across the country. The office in Denver had been hit the hardest, going from two hundred people down to twenty. During the day Ashley would circle technology jobs in the paper for me to look at when I got home. I applied for all of them and I called to follow up every time. If someone answered the phone, it was always the same response: "Be patient. We've received more than a hundred applications."

The first week of February five more people were let go. I went home that night, picked up the paper and saw no jobs circled. There was nothing. Late that night I sat holding Camryn asleep in my arms and listening to the news. There was a possibility that the United States might go to war with Iraq because they denied having weapons of mass destruction, but we thought they weren't telling the truth. I listened in disbelief for hours that the United States wanted to go to war because of a lie.

I put Camryn in her crib and climbed into bed next to Ashley and closed my eyes. My body was exhausted but my mind kept on until finally my body began to vibrate for the first time in nearly a year. I rolled over and headed for the back door, opened it and went outside. I spread my arms and jumped into the night sky as far up as I could. When I finally slowed down and looked below me I was over an island in the middle of the ocean with no other land in sight. It was daytime when I landed on the beach with no one around but my thoughts and me. Sitting at the edge of the water I watched as the clear waves slowly washed in, smoothing the sand before retreating back out to sea.

In the distance the silhouette of a person appeared along the edge of the water walking towards me. As this person moved closer, the daylight revealed it was a woman who appeared to be native to the island. She was wearing a long yellow and red sarong with beads wrapped around both of her wrists and she held out her arms to prepare for an embrace. I stood up and she did just that. With the sound of the waves lapping at the shore she held me by my arms, leaned back and with a smile she said, "Hello, Frank.

You've made it."

"Hi. Were you expecting me?" I asked.

"Tell me why you're here," she said, sitting down in the sand and gesturing to me to do the same.

"I'm just here to think."

"What are you here to think about?"

"My life. I'm very confused right now about what to do. I feel trapped."

She cupped her hand and scooped up some sand and held it in front of me. "This is your life."

"My life is a handful of sand?"

"Yes. It is made up of many small grains and no two are alike. Some are smaller than others and some are brighter than others. Together they are one. Each day of your life is like a grain of this sand and no single grain can define you."

"What do I do when the grains all start looking like fear?"

"There's only one thing you can do. Run," she said.

"Run? Run away?"

"Only you can decide which direction you choose to run," she said and smiled.

"Did you come here to tell me that?"

"No." She held out a folded white piece of paper. "I came here because I was asked to give you this. I was told you would know what it means."

"Thank you," I said. I took the paper, unfolded it, and saw just a single word written on it: "Breathe."

Since we are only part of the physical world temporarily, it would make sense that other realities exist for us to experience. Our minds appear to be capable of creating a reality beyond the physical world for us to experience that is similar to the world as we know it, which makes it possible that our reality is just an extension of that ability. If all living things have collectively agreed at some level that the physical world does exist, then in fact it is our agreement that makes it a reality. If this is true, then reality may not be real at all – a possibility that seems more plausible than a physical world that exists without our involvement and we are limited by our temporary existence within it. Perhaps we are born into this world because we gave birth to it.

IX

INTENTION

When we lose our direction we find our way.

Our minds are the bridge between what is and what will be, and our intentions are the hands that we use to shape the world around us. We can change them or deny them, but they cannot be escaped. When we consider all the pieces of us that we project onto the world, we cannot escape the fact that our actions shape the world. The paths that present themselves guide us, but choice determines our destination. Where we arrive is a function of all actions prior to the final moment before we make that decision. It is at that point that thought and intention create something out of nothing. It was time for me to start taking risks to further test the strength of my beliefs.

I took the advice that was given to me and I dealt with my fear by running straight at it. I decided to quit my job before it could quit on me and start my own business. At the same time Ashley and I also decided to have another child. Camryn was getting close to four years old and we thought it was time. We converted our single car detached garage into an office and the walk-in closet off our bedroom into a nursery. These two decisions seemed to defy common sense at that time in our lives, but we became empowered by our will to not live in fear. Our intentions were only to improve our circumstances, and our efforts to make it work filled us with excitement we hadn't felt in two years. We stopped waiting and took control of our lives.

It didn't take long before I began getting contract jobs to build websites and applications. A couple of guys I knew had a small company and were looking for someone to help build a website for a truck stop. When that was complete we built another site for a diving club. Within a few months word of mouth spread, and I developed a wide range of my own clients. I managed the networks for several hotels and wrote the software that managed two law firms in California. I also built websites for a lot of smaller clients, then eventually started my own web hosting service, providing everything a small business would need to get started. After six months I began making significant profits, but more importantly I had plenty of work to keep me busy for a year.

It was the middle of the fall of 2003 when Ashley walked slowly into the garage where I was sitting at my desk and said, "It's time to go."

We arrived at the hospital and began the familiar process of bringing a new life into the world. Ashley went through a few waves of pain then received relief when the anesthesiologist arrived and inserted a long needle between the vertebrae in her lower back leaving a thin tube in her spinal cord. We chatted into the night while her contractions increased, bringing us closer to a new life that would soon be in our care. The following morning we were handed a healthy newborn baby, we named her Erin and our family was complete. She started as a thought and less than a year later we were grateful to have her as a reality.

I began working long hours to keep up with the contracts that were coming in. Some nights I'd fall asleep at my desk or not sleep at all. Other nights I would put my head back and close my eyes to rest for a moment and when I opened my eyes my body would start vibrating. I'd stand up, walk out into my backyard take two steps and project into the sky. This routine allowed me to gain tremendous amounts of information by traveling to different locations and talking with anyone who was willing. Over the next few months I began to notice a few significant changes taking place. When I returned from information gathering and opened my physical eyes, my body would continue to vibrate until I focused my mind back on my work. My need for sleep and food began to diminish significantly while I was still able to function normally. The creativity around my work also improved, and I was solving problems much quicker than I ever had in the past.

After a few months of this routine I experienced a change that I wasn't expecting while meeting with one of my customers.

"Good to see you, Frank. Come in. I can't wait to see the website."

"Great to see you, Jack. I think you're going to like it. How've you been?" I asked.

"Tired," he said, moving slowly towards the chair in front of him and lowering himself down. Jack had back cancer and he was in quite a bit of pain. "How's business?" He asked in rough dry voice, holding out his hand to shake mine.

"It's been good," I said. I reached out to take his hand and felt a vibration that quickly ran up my arm. My ears began to ring and when I shook his hand I felt numb for a moment until we let go. I must have looked puzzled because Jack asked me if I was alright.

"I'm good. Let's look at this website," I said standing beside him opening my laptop. The vibration quickly faded and the meeting continued as planned.

When I arrived back to my home office I found the classified ads sitting on my keyboard with a pink Post-it stuck in the center. It read – "You're working too many hours. Love you. Ashley!" I pulled the note from the paper and under it was a circled job posting for a network analyst at Chipotle. My first thought was that I loved Chipotle. It was a small burrito chain that started in Denver near the University of Denver with a store where I'd had Chipotle for the first time when I moved to Colorado. I ate there several times a month for years, and when I met Ashley she was also a big fan and we starting eating there once a week. I went into the house and Ashley was sitting on the couch with Erin on her lap smiling and kicking her legs because she was glad to see me. I walked over, leaned in to kiss Ashley then scooped Erin off her lap with one hand and held out the other with the Post-it stuck to my finger.

"If it's less hours and free burritos, we're set," I said.

She clapped her hands together, smiled and said, "I've heard it's a really fun place to work too."

"I'm all for fun." I said.

I started with Chipotle in July of 2004 when the company had about 400 locations and was still owned by McDonalds. The headquarters was in downtown Denver on Wazee Street in a building that was constructed in the late 1800s. My first day on the job, I walked off the elevator and was greeted by a yellow Lab with a Post-it Note stuck to his back that read: "My owner doesn't feed me. I need some food!" The ceiling was all exposed with original wooden beams and the exterior walls were red brick. The work cubicles were open and positioned to allow for maximum conversation and everywhere you looked people were grouped in conversation about Chipotle. The standard dress code at the time was jeans (rips optional), a multi-colored Chipotle t-shirt with cool marketing, and the most fashionable shoes you could find. There were obviously variations to this attire, but one thing no one varied on was working hard and loving Chipotle. And yes, we all got free burritos.

After a year and half of working in my garage, I had found a new place to work where I was part of something bigger than myself. Just after my second week I learned how much I was about to get involved, when the head of technology walked up and sat on my desk, which was a common practice at the time, and asked, "Your resume said you can program?"

"Correct."

"I need you in a meeting right now."

"Let's go," I said.

We walked up to the meeting room just as two Secret Service agents were walking out. I knew instantly we were meeting with people from McDonalds because the other people in the meeting were wearing suits. They turned out to be attorneys who specialized in credit card fraud.

"We've had a possible breach of credit card information and we're interested to know if you could look at the point of sales system and see if there's a way to create a temporary fix while the software company works on a permanent solution?"

"I can look at it and let you know."

"Great. Please don't discuss this with anyone. Thanks," he said, and the meeting was over.

Over the next few days I got to my know my team very quickly. It was a small team of about fifteen, and we immediately began working sixteen-hour days to solve the stolen credit cards issue while keeping everything else running. At the time we were averaging one restaurant opening a week and our staff was increasing rapidly to support our growth. My responsibility was to write a program to delete all credit card information including the moment it was created at any of the hundreds of locations in multiple states. That was the start of my third week at Chipotle.

I worked sixteen hours a day for five days straight, writing a program to look for credit card information on a computer several times a second and delete it immediately. The program worked on our lab system so we decided to give it a try. At midnight on the last day of my third week the program was deployed to all locations and began deleting credit card information. Some of us slept in our chairs for a while, others went home to get a few hours of sleep so they could relieve the rest of us in the late morning. Ashley picked me up from work at lunch time because I was too tired to drive myself home.

"How did it go?" she asked as I got into the passenger seat wearing my Chipotle t-shirt and carrying my blue tennis shoes.

"Holy crap! I've never been happier in my life."

I spent a lot of time at work in the early years, but I still found time for my family and to work with my vibrations and finally decided to look outside of myself for validation. The logical first choice was Ashley. She always supported me in everything I talked about no matter how odd it seemed at the time. It started with me offering a massage as I sent vibrations to my hands then it would turn into a session of "can you feel that?" The first time I tried she turned over and said, "How did you do that? I felt that!" That was how it began.

I would try all the time. Hold my hands over her stomach or over her head. She would always respond by saying, "That's pretty cool." One time she had a head cold and I put my hand over her forehead and began to pull and push against something that felt like a magnet around her head. I could feel a force stronger than in the past. There was something pulling back against me. Then I tried to push it instead and go with the flow. Within a few minutes she sat up in hurry to run to the bathroom because her sinuses quickly began to drain. I always wanted to believe her when she said she felt something when I put my hands over her head. But a part of me always wondered if she was just playing along since it was actually hard for me to believe it as well. When her sinuses actually cleared I began to believe in the possibility that holding my hand above her I really was feeling her energy. The "magnet" sensation was actually in my hand as if something was pulling or pushing against it.

I came up with an experiment one night and I asked Ashley if she wouldn't mind being my subject. She stood directly in front of me facing forward in our hallway with her back to me. Both walls of the hallway were lined with pictures of the kids in silver frames.

"Okay," I said. "Look straight forward and with your peripheral vision I want you to keep an eye on the picture frames."

I put my hands on either side of her head and I could feel the magnets around my hands within seconds. I began to push the magnet with my left hand as I pulled with my right. I was trying to create a shift in her energy that might distort the picture frames the way heat waves on the pavement distort the look of the buildings behind it. After about sixty seconds she began to lose her balance and she fell backwards into my arms.

"Okay, I need a minute," she said. "That was weird. I can feel you pull me backwards."

That was the first time I sensed she was not pleased with what had just happened.

"You pulled me over." It was at that point she requested a break from the energy work and I was on my own again.

Four months after starting with Chipotle I went to the mountains with everyone in the IT department to spend time together and talk about what we could do to make the company better. At night we all went out and had a few drinks. Steve Ells, the founder of Chipotle, met us up there on the second night and when I saw him sitting at the bar, I went up and sat next to him and introduced myself.

"Hello, I'm Steve." He said holding out his hand and looking me straight in the eye through his thick framed glasses as he shook my hand.

In my excitement I immediately asked, "At what point did you know Chipotle had made it?"

He gave me an extremely confused look and said, "Are you saying this is as good as it gets? Is it over?"

"That's a great point," I said.

"We're changing the way the world thinks and we're just getting started," he said with great confidence.

I had an instant respect for Steve as a leader and a visionary. Everyone at Chipotle was there to work hard and we all got along because we shared the same goal. Every day revolved around how to manage the company's increasing growth and success. I felt honored to go to work because I believed in our mission, I believed what we were doing was making the world a better place, and I believed in Steve.

The week I returned from the mountains, my daughter Camryn developed an ear infection. We had an appointment to take her to the doctor and had given her some over-the-counter medicine for the pain but late that night she was up crying. In attempt to calm her down I carried her while humming and rubbing her back. It didn't seem to help and as any parent would be, I was willing to try anything. I set her in front of me and smiled then cupped my hand over her ear and began to feel for her energy. After a few moments I felt the sensation, and with her still crying I began to push and pull against the magnet I felt around my hand. She kept crying and I felt a little ridiculous so I picked her back up, but her crying slowed and she quickly fell asleep on my shoulder. I chalked it up to her being so tired and seeing me there smiling for a moment had provided some distraction, allowing her to fall asleep. I did find it interesting that I was willing to try something like that at that time.

Several days later I received an email from, Robert Bruce, an author whom I had written to six months earlier. His book was about meditation and out-of-body experiences and had helped me better understand the vibrations I felt and better ways to meditate. "G' day," began the email from him that changed my life just a little bit. He told me his mother had died, causing the delay in his response. He apologized and then got down to business. "I've heard of this type of thing before. You are experiencing kundalini."

It was that simple to him. What I felt was real and had a name, and he gave me advice. I exchanged emails with him, asking and receiving his answers to the best of his knowledge. I tried not to bother him too much and he responded within hours every time. I looked on his website one day to discover he was going to be in Helena, Montana, doing a program, and I decided to go see him without any other intent than to personally say, "Thank you." Ashley encouraged me to go and I began the twelve-hour drive.

What I found when I arrived was a group of twenty others who were there to find something more. From around the country and all very well read, they had backgrounds ranging from software developers to career mothers. An actor and his assistant were there; another woman worked for the county. We were all there to see Robert, but with the added benefit of meeting each other and knowing we were not alone.

I got to know Robert quite well over the next few days. We were all sitting around a bonfire and chatting amongst ourselves when Robert walked over to me and sat down. The orange flickering glow from the fire lit up his profile and as he turned to look directly at me from the shadow I could see only the white of his eye. He put his hand on my shoulder and said, "You're a healer. Have you ever put your hands on someone with cancer?"

As you can imagine, this was not what I was expecting. I looked at him and said "Are you serious?"

"There's one thing I can tell you. You need to help others," he said. "*How* is entirely up to you."

The next morning I got up from my bunk bed, packed the last of my clothes into my bag and walked through the dining area and out through the old screen door. Out back everyone was gathered to say their goodbyes. I have to admit their kindness surprised me. We, all of us, had experiences that were not out of this world but very much part of this world. We had all been brought together at a point in time to share what we knew and express what we could not understand. I promised to keep in touch but I knew I would not; they promised to do the same but they did not. This path is one you walk alone, though from time to time you come to an intersection and if you're lucky others like you are there to connect.

Working for Chipotle proved to be one of those paths that I was meant to follow. One year after I started I went to a meeting with several people from McDonalds, and I listened as we discussed separating all the Chipotle systems from the McDonalds systems because Chipotle was going to go public on the New York Stock Exchange. Over the next year and a half everyone did their part to get us prepared for that day. It was an exciting time in all of our careers; some of us saw success in our future while some thought we were selling out and quit. I saw it as a time to learn.

My team's responsibility was to build duplicate systems to process everything, build an accounting center, and become Sarbanes Oxley compliant. We worked long days and several team members began having to travel to Columbus, Ohio, to work on the accounting center. Pressure was high with extremely short deadlines and a very small team but we were all in it together so we enjoyed every minute. We eventually separated every system, created a fully functioning accounting center and became what's affectionately known as SOX compliant. Everything we needed to do to go public was completed by everyone working together.

Ashley and I took out a loan to buy as many stock options as we were allowed. When I got to work on the day we went public I found an envelope on my desk with more options and a note, thanking me for all of my hard work and signed by Steve Ells. Everyone had envelopes on their desk and we were streaming the opening of the New York Stock Exchange from our desks to watch Steve ring the bell. Ashley and I texted all day while we watched the market, and by the time I got home that night our investment had doubled. We were extremely grateful, and all of the time and effort we had invested and the decisions we had made began to pay off in a way we had neither expected nor focused on. We became financially secure and had a great family.

I've heard the expression "The point of no return." I reached that point while I was at my daughter's soccer game. I was informed Craig, a dad of a girl on the team, was dying from cancer. In fact, the way it was stated to me was not "if" but "when," and he'd been given less then six months. I remember looking at him talking with his daughter on the sideline and all I could think was it just wasn't fair. This dad and daughter were about to have a different story than was planned – a story filled with grief. That's when I crossed that line. Distraught at the thought of this family's future, I decided to try to do the ridiculous.

Being the logic-based guy I am, I began to try to work out in my mind a way living energy could help someone heal themselves. It stands to reason that a sudden energy increase could slow time down dramatically for a person's body, allowing for a brief moment of time where disease and illness appear to slow in growth. If true, it's plausible the body could gain an immediate advantage due to the already heightened battle internally within the body to cure itself.

At soccer practices, I would sit and look at Craig and his family and I would try to imagine what it would be like to be in their situation. But it was too difficult to imagine. Then I would try to justify why it was happening and create an excuse for "why this family and not mine" – but I could not. Then one Saturday during one of the games I looked at him and could not stop thinking about how unfortunate his situation was. Suddenly my hands began to vibrate to a point I could feel them shake. I was well aware of what was happening – and I knew I was going to try to do something so I would at least never have the regret. The game ended and the closing ceremonial tunnel created by the parents of the children began. I lined up across from the him to wait for the kids to come running in our direction. A calm washed over me as he held up his hands and I reached out to press my palms to his. I knew he would never know what I was trying, which made it less threatening to attempt. In a single second I could feel the vibrations run up my arms and into my hands. I worried that he could feel my hands shake so I pulled away slightly so we were no longer touching. To my surprise he reached forward and grabbed onto my hands and did not let go.

I could feel a current run through my body and into my hands until the tunnel ended a few moments later and our arms fell away. I clasped my hands together and realized he was doing the same. He was holding his wrist of his right arm and rubbing it back and forth. Not once throughout the experience did we make eye contact or speak.

I scooped up my daughter and headed back to our car. The experience had overwhelmed me to a point that I turned to Ashley and told her that my forearm hurt and oddly enough it was from vibrations. She responded as she always did without great reaction but just enough acknowledgement that I knew she was listening. Then we drove home and not another word was spoken or thought about it.

Two weeks had passed and I was standing in our kitchen holding Erin upside down blowing on her stomach and just as I put her down Ashley said, "You're not going to believe this but I just heard Craig's cancer is gone."

I heard a bang and then there was a loud ringing in my ears. My knees began to buckle as I reached out to grab on to the kitchen counter to steady myself. I believe I said, "No way," one or two times then walked into the living room and sat down.

She walked over to me and said, "Is this what you were telling me in the car after the game?"

"Not even close," I said.

A few weeks later at soccer practice Craig was there and I'd never seen him happier. He and his wife were telling everyone of their great fortune and he was going to be okay. One of the parents asked how they found out. His wife responded by saying, "We're still in shock. We were trying to make peace with the fact that he was going to die and then he was well." She hesitated for a moment looking at Craig then said, "The doctors couldn't explain how it happened. We think we willed it. He healed himself." Everyone listening nodded with agreement.

That experience did not validate anything in my mind. It only allowed me the freedom to further question what is real and what is possible. The vibrations I experience are because I've chosen to focus on them and through years of practice I've learned to move them throughout my body at will. This ability is in no way unique to me and I've met many people can do the same. Its also something anyone could do if they made their understanding/energy a focus in their life.

Exploration is critical to our success. If we push ourselves to continually redefine what is real we'll slow time by increasing our understanding of the world around us, providing us with greater clarity. Within our clarity we see purpose and we define who we are and the value of our life. We each define our individual purpose through freedom of choice and the karma that will determine the life we live.

X

Purpose

Change begins the moment we imagine it.

Purpose is a dot on the horizon where understanding and vision meet. It is here where we string small bits of understanding together with imagination to turn possibilities into realities. Imagination is the preliminary process to creating a vision. Uncovering the logic embedded in the imaginative idea is the practice towards creating vision. And once you have a vision, you have the ability to influence that path to the future that we call "purpose." Purpose is the greatest strength we possess. It's stronger than muscle, conquers all fear, and its effects defy time.

In pursuing our purpose we can knowingly make adjustments based on the impact an experience has on how quickly time passes. If time appears to pass more quickly, we know our growth of understanding is increasing. Throughout my life's journey, discovering the relationship between different events, experiences and people consistently provided me a clear understanding – a key factor in the equation to determine purpose.

Understanding is an energy we can feel if we use our body as an instrument to measure fluctuations in time during interactions with others. When associating ourselves with those of similar beliefs a dramatic slowing of time occurs making time appear to move faster. Knowing my purpose accelerates my understanding, creates greater clarity in my life, and provides a clear path to the future.

In order to gain a clear picture of my purpose, I chose to challenge my beliefs; essentially debating myself. This questioning and exploration is a necessary process enabling further perspective, justification and sometimes a shift or modification to a choice validating a more compelling reality. Once a true path is defined, we are no longer held hostage by our current situation, and the growth of understanding becomes our guide.

Through our efforts together, Ashley and I achieved a level of success that made us feel emotionally safe and financially secure. This achievement awarded me the time to reflect on my life and the people who inspired me to be a better person through their willingness to share their understanding of the world with me. Many people came to mind, and of all of those people, the ones who experienced and achieved things I deemed impossible for myself not only impressed me but inspired me to rid myself of doubt and fear, instead challenging myself to go out and make a difference.

One such person was the man with black lung whom I had met when working for the medical company. I was twenty-four years old at the time that he told me of being an avid mountain climber in his younger years. He'd climbed the likes of Longs Peak, an iconic mountain and considered to be the most difficult third-class fourteener in Colorado, Mt. Rainier in Washington State, and even Mt. McKinley in Canada. I clearly recall thinking to myself what amazing accomplishments they were – and ones that seemed impossible for me to replicate. He used the story of his youthful climbs as a paradox to his then life, barely able to take a step without losing his breath. Instead of being depressed by the comparison, he viewed his condition as a new mountain to climb. His story became the starting point in my journey to define my purpose – the motivation I needed to begin to climb my mountain, literally and figuratively.

A number of my fellow Chipotle team members were hikers, and many talked about climbing regularly, often climbing to the top of Colorado's many fourteen-thousand-foot peaks. Intrigued by the idea, I discovered that several people were planning a trip for the following month. They invited me to come on the trip, but warned me it was not going to be easy.

Over the next month we met regularly and they went over what we would need to summit the mountain. The most important necessity was to bring at least two liters of water, which along with warm clothes would be added weight I wasn't looking forward to carrying. Any additional weight becomes even more difficult to carry as the air thins, containing less oxygen, as you climb in altitude. The air also contains less moisture as you ascend, which means your outward breathing contains more moisture than what you breathe in, causing quicker dehydration. We needed the water to stay hydrated in order to avoid altitude sickness, which begins with dizziness and drying of the mouth and can lead to severe headaches and vomiting if not addressed properly.

In an attempt to make my experience as successful as possible I bought some hiking boots and the lightest warm clothes I could find. Every morning for four weeks I got up before sunrise and ran for a few miles to help with my conditioning. The sun rose midway through my run each morning, casting its bright light on rooftops and washing over the trees that lined my path to a park in our neighborhood. As I entered the park, the trees opened up to reveal a large clearing of grass where off in the distance every morning I would see a man throwing a tennis ball to his dog in front of a backdrop of the Rocky Mountains on the horizon, bathed in the morning light.

Saturday arrived and my alarm went off at four a.m. I rolled over and kissed Ashley goodbye, put on my boots, picked up my backpack and water, and headed for the mountains. We drove to the trailhead which started just less than twelve-thousand feet above sea level, leaving us with more than two-thousand feet to hike up over a distance of four miles. It was a clear day and the weather was warm with a forecast of clear skies all day. The conditions were perfect – thankfully.

The start of the climb was much like a walk through the woods with large trees lining a flat rocky path. After we'd walked for ten minutes, the trees began to thin out revealing several peaks in front of us as we were walking on a hillside. The path began to curve and elevate at the same time. The mountains around us didn't appear to be too difficult until the path started to rise more quickly, as did my heart rate and breathing. We followed the hillside path for a few more minutes until directly in front of us we could spot the mountain we were going to climb just a mile in the distance. This mountain dwarfed the peaks we had just passed with patches of snow most of the way up and the top, a massive pile of boulders. It was at that moment that I began to reflect on my decision and the reality of what I was about to embark on started to sink in. It was going to take a lot of effort for us to make it to the top.

After ten or fifteen minutes more of heavy breathing my mouth became dry and I began to drink one of the two large containers of water I had strapped to the side of my backpack. Over the next two hours I became increasingly fatigued and my pace slowed significantly. It was easy for me to see my friend ahead of me on the trail. All I had to do was look up. Every step we took up was a rise of at least six inches, and at times I had to pull myself up on large rocks on either side of the trail to take the next step. The trek was exhausting and progressively getting more difficult as we passed some of the large patches of snow we had seen from the distance to realize they were actually large sheets of ice. It was at that point that I sat down on a boulder, looked back to where I had come from and thought how easy it would be to just turn around and head back down. Then I thought of the man with black lung who had inspired me to do this climb, and suddenly I gained a surge of energy to tackle the remainder of the trail head on.

I decided that rest on the boulder would be my last break until I reached the top, and I began to climb again. Each step was an event in itself. I had to look at the rocks to see where to step so I wouldn't slip, and each time I lifted my body closer to the top I did so with a single exhale. I began to hear my heartbeat in my ears and the sweat from my forehead stung my eyes as the sun hung high overhead pouring itself down on the mountain. As I arrived closer to what appeared to be the top, I was aiding every step by pulling myself up on the rocks around me. When I finally reached the top my friend was standing there waiting for me. A feeling of victory flowed through my body that I had finally caught up with him and we made it to the top – only to learn we weren't there yet.

"You ready?" he asked.

"Ready for what?"

"That." He pointed at a peak that was slightly higher than we were, with a narrow path leading to it. Both sides of the path quickly fell away, exposing frighteningly deep valleys below. "You can easily walk across it," he explained. "It's actually about thirty feet wide, but when you're standing in the middle of it you feel like you're on a tightrope."

"Good to know." I said with a nervous laugh.

"Feel free to crawl if its starts to get windy or you start to get nervous."

"Sold," I said. We snapped our helmets on and started walking towards the peak. The path in front of us was a solid piece of rock with large grooves cutting into it vertically, making it look narrower than it really was. I walked slowly forward, looking down at every step I took, but my breath was slow and my heart was calm. Midway across I stopped and looked at the edges of the path. Nothing but blue sky showed on either side of me and for a moment it seemed as if I was floating in the sky. A rush of energy filled my body with vibrations and a smile from down inside of me surfaced as I felt joy mixed with relief. I held my arms out like wings and looked at the sky all around as we moved with ease across the path. At the end of the path I had to lift myself up one last time to see my friend sitting on a rock with nothing but blue sky all around him and a smile on his face.

"Welcome to the top of the world," he said, gesturing into the sky. As I walked closer the scene behind him unfolded, revealing mountain ranges in the distance below us. The world stretched as far as the eye could see with a crystal blue backdrop illuminating its peaks.

I stood for a moment just breathing in the cold mountain air and my mind began to drift into the distant horizon as the child in me rose to the surface. A child who once hid in a box had found his way to the top of the world. With my lungs filled with the cool thin air, I shouted, "I am here!"

After a few pictures there was nowhere else to go but home. Getting down is extremely easy in comparison to going up, but it still wasn't as easy as I had thought it would be. Still, climbing that first fourteener made me want to push myself to have more challenging experiences with greater purpose. I continued to climb and even decided to add a marathon to my repertoire of experiences I never believed possible.

It didn't take much longer to realize that I needed more to define my purpose in pursuing the future. I began to desire a purpose beyond myself and my family, creating a positive influence on the world around me. It was time for me to change my world.

At that time the economy once again took a turn for the worse but fortunately Chipotle was still doing well. During some of the most difficult months of the recession we were still opening several new stores a week all around the country. Chipotle was an amazing concept created by a brilliant man and I was grateful for every moment I was a part of it. I loved my job and my family didn't have to worry about losing our income. In keeping with my gratitude for my circumstances I felt an obligation to work as hard as I could to help keep Chipotle successful.

My team with the company had grown considerably and began to spread out across the country to support the technology. This growth changed my job dramatically by adding the element of travel so I could get out and meet with my customers and team in person. It was a very exciting time for me since I hadn't seen much of the country, but the downside was being away from Ashley and the girls. When I started to travel I called them every night and we'd talk for twenty minutes before the girls went to bed, but over time it became difficult. The more I traveled the less we talked at night – and some nights we didn't talk at all, just texting a quick, "Good night. Love you."

I traveled light as I flew from Boston to the Bay Area and anywhere in between – sometimes visiting several cities in the same week. Headphones and my iPhone were most important to my survival, delivering flight notification, directions to hotels, making calls, and most importantly, providing music for the long and lonely stretches of time I spent waiting.

Another aspect of my job that changed a bit was interviewing. I began interviewing every potential new employee to ensure they'd be a great cultural fit for my team before hiring them. The criteria new hires needed to meet continued to be set higher; each person had to be highly motivated and technically sound or they weren't going to last long at Chipotle. By this time we were a team of ninety and we were running lean. An average work week was fifty-five hours and we worked hard every minute. Our continued growth required us to hire more staff, but very few qualified people were looking for jobs and our workload continued to grow. This deficit of candidates astounded me as at the time unemployment was at an all-time high. I knew I needed to do more to keep us moving forward.

I decided to expand my network of people in the local technology community to see if I could find some qualified people to fill our open jobs. I attended an event held by the Colorado Technology Association where their CEO, Steve Foster, was speaking about developing the technology workforce of tomorrow and the challenges of finding qualified people. During his talk he mentioned that high school graduation rates were slightly over fifty-percent, a contributing factor to the gap in our workforce. I was stunned by the statistic and walked up to him after his talk and asked if there was a way I could learn more about this issue.

"We have an education committee that meets every month. Would you be interested in attending?" he asked.

"Absolutely," I said. "What would I be doing?"

"You're running it. I'll send you an email," he said, then patted me on the back and walked away.

It was the beginning of yet another chain of reaction events that I had set in motion by opening my eyes to a societal challenge I never knew existed. If fifty-percent of kids in large city schools are not graduating from high school, we are losing half of the next generation of brilliant minds. In a world where *understanding is the energy that constitutes life*, limiting the opportunities for children slows our potential for growth as a peaceful and prosperous civilization. Limiting potential opportunities also limits our perspective as a society, creating fractures in our collective understanding and dividing us as individuals.

I felt obligated to better understand why high school dropout rates were so high and began attending meetings held regularly on behalf of Colorado Technology Association. Soon I was meeting with educators, state senators, lobbyists and nonprofits and was eventually asked to testify on a third-grade reading proficiency bill before the state senate. The bill addressed the statistical reality that children who can't read at grade level by third grade will drop out of high school.

A week later I was asked to speak on panel at Aurora Public Schools (APS) during a visit from Arne Duncan, the Secretary of Education under President Obama. APS high school graduation rates were just above fifty-percent and the school system was looking to local businesses for help. I spoke with John Barry, the Superintendent of Schools for Aurora, and after the event he said they were looking for professionals to donate their time to help mentor the kids to keep them in school. At the time, I was traveling nearly every week and spending less time with my family, but somehow I knew I needed to make this school and business coalition work as I saw that teamwork as critical to our future. I brokered a relationship between Aurora Public Schools, MapQuest and Noodles & Company on behalf of Colorado Technology Association, and we created a mentorship program named "Project Kick Off." The program attracted 21 students and involved six companies and a State Senator.

On one of my week-long trips for Chipotle, I read Michael Moore's book that ends with him taking a risk leading to the premiere of his first documentary. The idea of creating a film to make a point appealed to me so much that I decided to make a short documentary bringing attention to

211

low high school graduation rates while providing a solution at the same time. We filmed the creation and the process of "Project Kick Off" and produced a documentary titled "Moving Mountains." The film was shown at a CTA event with over twelve-hundred in attendance including the twenty-one kids from the Aurora Public Schools mentorship program. Camryn came to the event and was in the audience with me when the film began. I held my breath as I looked around the audience in the massive banquet hall, and within the first five minutes nearly everyone was engaged until the end. At the conclusion of the film I walked up on stage along with the kids from the program and John Barry. The massive hall erupted with applause and we received a standing ovation. As the applause roared on I could see Camryn smiling in the distance waving to me and it became clear to me what I needed to do next.

That night Ashley and I sat on our balcony and talked for hours about the event, the program, the kids, and the future. We talked about our kids and how lucky we felt in our lives and our obligation to give back. If we could invest more time to show the next generation a future with many opportunities it would enrich their future by increasing their perspective and help them define their paths. It was idealistic talk, but it's what we believed to be true. An increased investment in the next generation would enrich their future with a greater understanding of the world around them and of each other, providing them with hope and purpose.

"What you're talking about is a holistic generation," Ashley said, "where everyone works together and sacrifices to improve the lives of the next generation, making goals more tangible and making the world more prosperous for everyone."

"Yes," I said. "A Holistic Generation." She's brilliant.

The world around us begins to get more interesting as well as more difficult based on the decisions we've made to alter our future. Sharing understanding alters the future of all living things by opening new paths and increasing awareness. The idea would be to start a chain reaction of positive events that result in the betterment of the next generation. But we still have an obligation to those continuing to struggle due to the effects of previous generations – such as families who suffered tremendous loss during an economic downturn or those separated for long periods of time, or forever, because of war. It is for all of those people who have made voluntary and involuntary sacrifice that we should feel obligated to do more. In our actions we can find purpose knowing that we gave back as much as we could.

Purpose has a direct effect on reality. If we shift our focus to accomplishing as many goals as we can that we once believed unrealistic, we would start expanding our belief of what's possible. Those accomplishments would generate understanding, which is energy, slowing time for us exponentially. This progression would cause multiple effects. The creation of new energy resulting in a chain reaction of new paths for individuals that define their purpose. The result would be a positive perspective on the future by creating more options from which to choose. Multiple options means multiple points of view on reality, which in turn improves our focus and allows us to see the world with greater clarity.

As the chain reaction progresses, we'd be able to see trends of common realities shared by others, allowing us to further define our path and fine-tune our future. The effect this approach would have on a single individual could broaden their horizons by creating multiple paths to their desired state of reality.

Our ability to process information, which generates understanding/energy, also has a direct impact on our physical and mental states, allowing us to accomplish actions which we once believed unrealistic. The more information we have to associate, the greater our potential for understanding/energy growth.

The more individuals participating in an experience, the higher the energy level associated with that experience, which provides a greater potential for reality to expand in a given area. A perfect example of this process is civilization, which consists of a chain reaction towards the development of a peaceful existence through understanding. Hundreds of years in the future history will tell our generation's story, the one we're shaping today. Having clear purpose as an individual or as a society unlocks new possibilities and influences the future. Purpose shapes our future.

The following week, after eight and half years at Chipotle, I sent out an email saying, "Chipotle has changed my life and I gave it everything I had while I was here. Ashley and the girls have supported me working long hours, traveling and cancelling vacations when systems were down. It's now time for me to focus on them while trying to have a positive impact on the world around me just like I learned working with all of you."

Many people thought I was crazy to leave, especially at that time; walking away just three months before another big payout of my stock options was to become available. But somehow I knew this was the right time and it became clearer that a bigger payout of greater returns was on the horizon that wasn't measured in dollars. The equation of life coupled with a purpose to give what we can in the most selfless way to make the world a better place would be the start of a holistic generation.

While still staying heavily involved chairing the education committee for CTA, I went on a sabbatical to spend time with my family and to clear my mind. The first two weeks I spent my time with Ashley and the girls reconnecting and talking instead of texting. Ashley and I would go on long walks while the girls were in school and talk about our future. Some days we'd walk for hours and sometimes I'd walk alone, just thinking of new ideas of what I should be doing with my life.

It was fall and a time for a new beginning. I bought a guitar and started writing this book. Surprisingly I wasn't concerned about the future because I had a purpose and plenty of paths to choose from. One month into my sabbatical while walking through Washington Park with Ashley I received a phone call.

"Hello, is this Frank Daidone?"

"It is," I said.

"Hello, I'm calling from Mayor Michael Hancock's office. We're currently looking for a Chief Information Officer to run technology for the City and County of Denver. We're looking for someone who can really make a difference and we were given your name. Are you interested?"

My entire life and all of my experiences have prepared me for the most important moment, which is always right now. Focusing on the present allows me to be in complete control of who I am with the ability to absorb as much information as possible to fuel my growth. I immerse myself in experiences that challenge me beyond my current understanding and suddenly possibilities become endless.

I have had many relationships and experiences throughout my life and all of them, regardless of duration, have made me who I am at this very moment. I have now shared everything I know about *Life's Equation* and defining purpose. This book is my message in a bottle cast into the sea of hope.

"Anyone else out there?"

THE PAPER

UNDERSTANDING IS THE ENERGY WHICH CONSITITUES LIFE

Introduction

The following is a collection of observations that joined together could be labeled as the energy which constitutes life. To begin, I take into consideration that all living organisms contain the same form of energy regardless of their physical shape. Bacteria, humans and a single blade of grass all share a common trait in that their span of existence is limited. The following is not an attempt to explain consciousness but rather a volume of energy is associated with every living organism and is independent of what is contained within its physical existence. This energy is measurable and continues to increase as long as the organisms are in a state referred to as being alive.

Theory

There are three components to this theory. First, the physical world is made of individual objects joined together in specific combinations to create new objects. A good example would be H_2O molecules joined together to make a raindrop and that raindrop then falls in the ocean. I refer to these objects and their combinations as information. Information is the building blocks that generate living energy. Second, when experiencing events, senses become receivers of moments in time that are then associated in the mind, which results in greater understanding of reality. This process I refer to as Experience. Finally, the association of information though experience generates an energy I refer to as Understanding – the energy also known as life.

Equation

The association of two independent pieces of information via experience creates a reaction that results in the formation of new energy called understanding. An example would be touching a hot iron where hot and the iron are joined via touch resulting in the understanding of pain. That pain links those two bits of information and the energy derived from that experience gets stored in the form of understanding further increasing our energy level as a living thing, and that energy is "life."

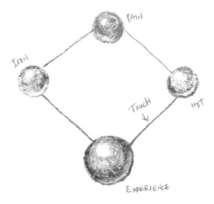

The more bits of information experienced during a given event, the richer the experience with a larger amount of energy created in the form of understanding.

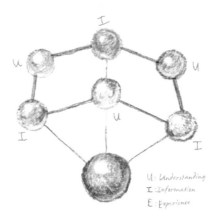

U: Understanding
I: Information
E: Experience

If the event has multiple forms of experience such as seeing and touching a glowing hot iron, then the amount of understanding that joins the bits of information will increase to create a stronger bond.

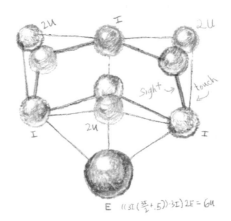

$$E \quad ((3I(\tfrac{E}{2}+.5))\cdot 3I)2E = 6U$$

A mathematical representation of the above would consist of three elements: Information (I), Experience (E), and Understanding (U) and it would look like this $((I\ (I/2 + .5)\ )-I)\ E = U$. Information is associated together multiplied by the number of ways it's experienced.

One of the functions of the brain is to act as an index to this understanding, like in the back of a textbook, allowing access to this energy as stored information in the form of memories. Understanding can then be viewed as information that allows the imagination to become another catalyst for understanding, much like the senses. The more information associated with a given memory, the more vivid the memory. With more memories there is greater potential to make associations, exponentially increasing the production of living energy. It is also possible to take a memory and maximize its potential by incorporating different perspectives, which then creates greater understanding. If this is in fact what living energy is, it could then also survive the destruction of the physical body. This energy coupled with new experiences enables constant growth and the rate of growth is only governed by desire to obtain new experiences and the ability to put oneself in a position to learn.

Measurement

Developing a sense of mutually "agreed upon time" is necessary to function in life and develop as a society. Agreed upon time is the equivalent to a common language of the physical world. As an example - five minutes is different than five hours, which is very different than five years. Measurement of agreed upon time can be accomplished by monitoring the movement of the sun or tides and more precisely by referring to a clock or stopwatch.

Due to the fact that understanding is a form of energy, it has a direct impact on time as explained by Einstein's Theory of General Relativity and the effects of gravitational time dilation. Gravitational time dilation is the effect of time passing at different rates in regions of different gravitational force. The larger gravitational force, the more slowly time passes. As an example - if you lived on Jupiter you would age more slowly than on Earth because the gravity around Jupiter is stronger therefore slowing time.

As an individual's understanding grows it dilates time slowing it down creating a perception for the individual that agreed upon time appears to be moving faster. A child's perception of agreed upon time is slower due to the low energy and mass content of the child. This allows a child to travel closest to agreed upon time. As an individual ages, and their energy and mass content increases, time dilation becomes greater, pulling the individual farther away from agreed upon time. The time dilation is what causes time to slow down for us as we age creating the perception agreed upon time is moving faster as we get older when in fact the time around us is moving slower.

Bonds between individuals and thoughts will also increase energy levels causing a more distinct change in the passing of time. This change takes place through the communication of ideas and the association memories. We continually recalibrate our internal time clock to compensate for energy growth, keeping us in synchronization with agreed upon time.

Conclusion

If understanding is living energy and is created in this fashion and can further be measured, then all livings things have a common bond. To increase this bond one may reach out to those around him/her and generate positive peaceful relationships through meaningful experiences. That approach allows opportunity for rapid growth in both oneself and the surrounding world respectively.

Made in the USA
Middletown, DE
24 January 2021